MW01166490

You Wouldn't Want To Be In My Shoes

by

D. D. Brantley

Bloomington, IN Milton Keynes, UK

AuthorHouse™
1663 Liberty Drive, Suite 200
Bloomington, IN 47403
www.authorhouse.com
Phone: 1-800-839-8640

AuthorHouse™ UK Ltd.
500 Avebury Boulevard
Central Milton Keynes, MK9 2BE
www.authorhouse.co.uk
Phone: 08001974150

© 2007 D. D. Brantley. All rights reserved.

*No part of this book may be reproduced, stored in
a retrieval system, or transmitted by any means
without the written permission of the author.*

First published by AuthorHouse 5/7/2007

ISBN: 978-1-4343-0879-5 (sc)

Printed in the United States of America
Bloomington, Indiana

This book is printed on acid-free paper.

Chapter 1

There is a *Miracle* called family that dwells within our hearts. You do not know how it happens or where it gets its start. However, the happiness it brings you always gives a special lift. In addition, you realize that family is God's sometimes imperfect but special gift.

My name is Angelica Denise Moore. I am going to take you on a journey into my world. Through all of the trials, tribulations, laughs and the cries. I'm a thirty-two year old single mother of three very different children. There's Denise who is seven and acts beyond her years. Cedric and Carlos are twins and at five years of age, they both think of themselves as my husband, since there is no significant man in my life at this particular moment. Cedric wants to tell me what to do most of the time, until I remind him of who the parent is. Carlos does not allow many men around me. I guess since I refuse to let what I went through as a child to happen to my kids, I therefore, sometimes appreciate Carlos bastion behavior when it comes to men.

This is my story, growing up I had two sisters and three brothers, Andrea who is two years older than me and my father's favorite, Shannon who is the youngest girl, Paul who is two years younger than Shannon, Damon who is two years younger than Paul, Melvin the baby is also two years younger than Damon. My dad; James left us when I was seven years old. My momma, Anne was a drunk and a very promiscuous woman. She would drink from sun up to sun down. Her drinking binges would go on for several days, even on Sundays. She cussed like a sailor; what ever came up came out of her mouth, and wouldn't care whose feelings she might of hurt.

Anne had no self-respect at all. I remember one day she said, "Angelica lets go to the store, get my purse, Andrea can stay with your sisters and brothers until we get back from the liquor store and make sure you lock the door." I hated to go to the liquor store with Anne because most of the men in the neighborhood knew that Anne was a drunk and they might have a chance to have fuck relations with her. "Anne where are you off to this fine morning?" said Mr. Smith who lived across the street. He had no children or a wife, and many women in the neighborhood found him repulsive, because he would try to have fuck relations with all women, even if they were married. Anne replied, "catch me when I come back," giving him a sexy smile and this is what I hated the most about Anne.

We went into the store; Anne bought some kind of cheap whiskey, what kind I don't remember, she then bought me and my brothers and sisters some chips, juice and candy. While walking back home from the store, Anne said "wait a minute." Wanting to get back home, I said, "what for?" she sneaked into the alley behind a building, pulled up her skirt only to discover that she had no panties on. She squatted down, then urinated right there in broad daylight. I noticed a green car pass us by with a man driving, only to back up and watch Anne peeing. Anne looked up and yelled, "what in the hell are you looking at? Haven't you ever seen someone take a piss before?" The man frowned and pulled off burning rubber by spinning the tires on his car. Anne pulled her skirt down and said, "come on let's go home I have some business to take care of." Therefore, I say once again, she had no self-respect.

We heard the doorbell ring. I and my brothers and sisters were ordered to the basement. There goes Anne playing the blues. As I think back, we had an old record player, the kind that had the television at the bottom. The record player was so worn out that you had to put a dime on the arm of the needle to prevent sliding across the record. It was brown in color and long, it reminded me of a casket that I was truly scared of. I remember coming in from school one day and the lid on the record player was up. I was smart enough to know that you associate dead people with caskets. I ran so fast to my parent's room just off the kitchen because I was so afraid that a dead body was going to rise up and grab me.

Mr. Smith came in and started singing, drinking and dancing with Anne. They were having such a good time; they were playing the music so loud that the windows in the basement rattled and we couldn't even hear them laughing nor talking. I was surprised that the neighbors didn't call the police. Then again, they were use to Anne's behavior. Suddenly there was silence and that's when I heard my parent's bedroom door close. A few moments later I hear dad come into the house, then all hell broke loose. "Anne what the fuck is going on in here, where are my children?" "James baby please don't be mad, he just came over for a drink." Bitch I am tired of this shit, I am leaving. "James don't, don't walk out on me and think of the kids." Damn it Anne you should have thought about the kids before you fucked this nigga. Moments later dad called out for us, we ran upstairs. He took us into the living room, sat us down and tried to explain to us that he was leaving, that he loved us and that his reason for leaving had nothing to do with us. He looked at Andrea and said, "You are the oldest and I expect you to take care of your sisters and brothers." Tears began to fall down her face and she said, "dad I will, but do you have to go?" Dad looked at all of us, cleared his throat and said, "Yes I have to go, I can't take your mother's behavior anymore." Dad then shouted, "Anne you no good bitch I should kill you and that nigga for fucking over my kids, but I know I would go to jail and never see my children again." Before Anne could get dressed and make it to the living room, dad had slammed the door, this would be the last time we would see him, so I thought. Mr. Smith walked out the front door with his head hanging low.

We begin to cry, oh that made Anne mad, "why in the hell are you crying?" Andrea being the oldest said "our dad is gone and I hate you, you are not a mother, you are a drunken whore and an embarrassment to all of us, how could you do this to our family." Andrea took us up to our bedrooms and closed our doors, leaving Anne standing there looking stupid. The words that they were using, I really didn't understand them. Moreover, with Andrea being the oldest, I wanted to ask her what they meant. I decided to keep my mouth shut.

Oh, lord there goes Anne playing those records again. From those days until now, I hate the blues. At one point and time Anne use to be a fine woman, she stood 5'2 and weighed about 110 pounds. She had the prettiest smooth brown skin.

After dad left, it was not hard for her to find another man. As long as she put out, and as long as they had plenty of money to supply her with whiskey and cigarettes, he was worth keeping. Mr. Smith was no longer in the picture. One night I heard Anne call him a cheap fucker, after him, there were so many men that Anne had brought into the house. We had to call them Uncle Bill, Uncle John; you get the point. I could not keep up with all those names so I just said "hi" and went on about my business. There was one in particular that I really didn't like named Billy.

Andrea is now thirty-four years old, she the biggest crack head in Detroit. When we were kids and her being the oldest, she said to me, "look at Anne, I will never drink, smoke cigarettes and for damn sure never do drugs." We never knew of Anne doing any kind of drugs but if she did, it wouldn't have surprised us at all. Andrea was a pretty girl, though the drug abuse had made her look older than what she really was. She stood 5'4, weighed 125 pounds, and had curves in all the right places. Crack cocaine really breaks the body down. Now she looks like ("hell riding on a motorcycle.") Andrea's skin is resembling ashen, a deadly pale in color. The pigmentation in her lips is beginning to turn colors; she now has pink spots on them.

Andrea married her junior high school sweetheart Tom Wilson at the age of eighteen. We were getting older, I was sixteen and Andrea had just turned eighteen three days after her high school graduation. The day after the graduation ceremony, Andrea told Anne that she was getting married in two weeks, she was tired of all the men and her drinking, and in the mean time she would be moving out. Anne in a drunken stupor manages to say, "Who gives a fuck, you can't come back here." Andrea didn't hear what Anne said, she was too busy upstairs in her room packing. When Andrea finished packing, she came downstairs to say her goodbyes. Andrea stood in the doorway of the kitchen and told Anne, "you need to keep that damn man named Billy out of this house, you have teenage girls living in this house and I think he's up to no good, and if I find out that he has said anything to Angelica and Shannon, you will be sorry." From that day forward, nothing else was ever mentioned about what Andrea said and with a blink of an eye, Andrea was gone.

I came in from the store one day. Anne was in the kitchen cooking dinner, that night we were having neck bones, pinto beans and hot water cornbread. "Angelica come here." I could tell that she had been drinking because her words were slurred. She said, "sit down, now look girl you know that Andrea has gotten married, and moved out; you are sixteen years old and your body is developing fast, these little nasty ass boys have been looking at you hard. Keep your damn legs closed and if you open them up, make sure that they pay for it. In this world you don't get something for nothing, do you hear me?" In a low whisper, I said, "I'm not having sex until I'm married." Anne being a smart ass said, "what ever." I stood up and walked out of the kitchen and Anne called me an ugly smart mouth bitch. Daughter like mother, I mumble to myself, I know you are but what am I.

Tom had so much going on for himself; he landed an electrical apprenticeship at the auto factory. After a year and a half on the job, a freak accident happens, Tom was struck in the back and neck by a hi-lo. With the injuries he sustained he was unable to return back to work, therefore that meant that Tom was out of work and on disability. He stayed in constant pain, so his doctor had to prescribe Violin 750mg, a new pain medication; he takes 1 tablet 3 times a day for his aches and pains.

Andrea was working at the post office as a mail carrier. Everything was fine and well with the two of them until while on her route, she was involved in an accident. A city bus broadsided her mail truck and the mail truck flipped over several times. The accident left Andrea on medical leave for several months; she retained an attorney and filed a lawsuit against the city. The bus driver admitted that he was in the wrong and the lawsuit was settled out of court. How much money she settled for, I have no clue. My nosy ass asked but she never told, I knew that the bitch got paid.

Andrea and Tom bought a house in the upscale part of town, called Builtmore Township. A house that was too large for the two of them, four bedrooms, two master bedrooms with private bathrooms, and three half bathrooms. It's not that much shitten in the world. Formal dining room that seats twelve with two chandlers, a library that had thousands of books that I knew they would never read, an indoor/outdoor swimming pool, a basketball court, a hot tub just off the patio by the kitchen door, and a circular driveway with two cars parked there that they didn't even drive. Andrea has a Mercedes Benz, and Tom had a BMW. This is just my opinion, they were living way beyond there means.

Now things were going well for them, until one Saturday night, Andrea calls me, "what's up my sista, and how are you doing?" "I'm fine and tired, just got finish playing with the boys, what's up?" Andrea was always in a cheerful mood. "Girl Buster is giving one of his off the chain parties, do you want to go?" I've never missed one of his parties. Knowing that I didn't have a babysitter, I had to tell Andrea that I couldn't go. She started to whine, "Oh Angelica I really want you to go, we haven't hung out in a long time." She even told me that Shannon might come. I gave Andrea a long sigh and said, "have fun for me." We said our goodbyes and I hung up the phone.

Denise comes running into the house out of breath, catching a second wind, she said, "mommy can I ask you a question?" Sitting down I knew how her question could be. "Sweet heart you know you can ask me anything," in a reassuring and calm voice. Denise dropped her head and said, "What does the word copulate mean and is it a bad word?" I went to sit beside her, trying to choose my words carefully, I inhaled, exhaled, and said, "That word is not a bad word and it means to have intercourse/sex." I wanted to know how she had come to hear this word. Gaining my composure, "who did you hear say this word?" "Some people were talking and when we walked up, they said that it was a shame that Mr. Smith and Billy were trying to copulate all the women on the street." "Never you mind Denise, you had no business standing there listening to grown folks talk, when you noticed that they were talking, you should have kept on walking, now go wash up and see what your brothers are doing." I swear that girl is too grown for me.

The kids had gone to bed and I was watching an old black and white scary movie on T.V., the telephone rung and scared the hell out of me. Picking up on one ring, "hello, hey Tammy what's up?" By me not being able to go to the party, my girls Tammy and Carla went. She told me that the party was all that and that I missed it. Even my two gay friends Anthony and Mark were there. Buster did not care that they were gay; he knew that they would bring the best weed with them. Tammy took a long pause and said, "Angelica there is no easy way to tell you this." I was afraid to ask. "Tammy what is it?" "Andrea and Tom went into one of Busters' bedrooms with a group of people. About twenty minutes later they all came out looking crazy. I soon found out that they were in the room smoking crack cocaine." I wanted to scream, but I couldn't form any words. "Someone went and told Buster, he threw all of them out and told them that this was not that kind of party, we were allowed weed and that was the only shit that would be allowed in his house." I just held the phone and listen to what all Tammy had to say. I begin to cry and said, "Tammy let me call you later on when I have time to absorb all of this."

Now there is my sister Shannon, she is altogether a different person. She's' thirty years old, she's an uppity bitch, and could be Anne's twin sister; at the age sixteen she graduated from high school, went on to college, receiving two master degrees, one in elementary education and the other in business management. Of course, she moved to the suburbs. Shannon felt that she was above living in the city. Driving her SUV truck, you couldn't hit her in the middle of her ass with a rotten red apple. I remember when we were kids; Anne was sitting on the front porch. "Come here Shannon, my pretty baby, hand me the telephone and tell your ugly ass sisters to keep that damn noise down." Shannon did not have a problem telling Andrea and myself just how ugly we were. Thumping Shannon on her forehead, I said, "If I am ugly so are you because we came out of the same pussy."

Shannon is dating a man named Michael who is some hotshot attorney. He has two offices, one in downtown Detroit and one in New York. He thinks he's the man because he has licenses to practice in five other states, Ohio, California, Georgia, Texas, and Alabama. With all that, he's ghetto as hell. In addition, just as sorry. Shannon was always a big dreamer; by the age of twelve, she had already planned her wedding. She told us her dress would be pure white and made of satin, with a nine foot train, her headpiece will have pearls and crystal accents; a house with the white picket fence, a dog, and many babies. Well they've been dating for the last five years and still no ring. One thing about Shannon that I didn't like, she would call me on the telephone and tell me what all she had bought for her condominium.

Our last conversation was about a month ago, she had brought my kids home after they spent the weekend with her. She comes bouncing her ass in my house. "Angelica I just went and bought myself the most beautiful Persian rug for the living room, this set me back for about six thousand dollars." "Damn Shannon why in the world would you spend that kind of money for a rug that you are going to lay on the floor?" Shannon became offended with an attitude, "do you think that I am that damn stupid and put a six thousand dollar rug on the floor? I'm going to hang it on the wall, and if I want to spend that kind of money on a rug, that's my damn business." Shannon and I could not be around one another ten minutes without having an argument. "Well look Shannon, I'm not telling you how to spend your money, but let me tell you this, you evil witch, what you have today can be gone tomorrow." Letting out an exasperating breath, Shannon put her hands on her hips, "fuck you, you're just jealous of me and all the things that I have and you wish that you could be just like me." She stormed out and slammed the door, which was the last time I had seen or spoken to her. For her to be a college graduate she is just plain stupid. I love her to death; I pray that she doesn't forget where she comes from. She'll never know who she's going to need one day.

Paul, my twenty eight year old brother is a walking nightmare. Anne failed him big time. Paul must have been about eight years old. The ice cream truck was coming up the street, he was running and hollering in the house, "Anne, Anne can I have money for an ice cream?" Anne was sitting in the chair in the den in a drunken sleep. Awakened by the hollering of Paul, giving him an evil look, Anne slapped him across his face so hard that it spun him around and he fell on the floor. He tried to cry but nothing would come out. "Give you some money for ice cream; I do not give little black bastards money for shit. If you let out one cry, I will whip your ass like there is no tomorrow, now take your ass upstairs to your room and do not come down until I call your name," Snarled Anne, then calling him "a little mother fucker." This left Paul in a trance, and traumatized him for years. I once heard that a person is a product of there environment. In addition, all the abuse that Paul endured as a child landed him in jail for domestic violence. You see Paul thinks that he can hit women and get away with it. He has everything going for himself, a good paying job as a computer programmer. He writes software for computers. Twenty-eight years old, stands 6'3, has the body of a Greek God and curly hair that men and women would die for. An outstanding dresser, look as if he just stepped out of a men's fashion magazine. Paul met his girlfriend Donna while she was standing at the bus stop. Paul being Paul, when he first saw her, did a u-turn in the middle of the street. Donna is cute, 5'8 in height, light skinned with short hair and average looking features. I've seen him with better. There was only one thing that I couldn't stand about Donna; she was dumb as a bag of rocks. Whatever Paul said, that was the law.

Donna came over to the house one day, and I noticed that she had a black eye. Horrified as to what I was looking at, I demanded to know, "Donna what the hell happen to you?" She confessed to me that Paul had been beating on her. I had an idea that this was going on but I had no way of proving this theory. Then to, this was none of my business. I was becoming very irritated with Donna, "why didn't you call the police?" "Angelica I love Paul so much, I know that he was frustrated with work and I had been nagging him about taking the garbage out. In addition, I know about the abuse that he went through as a child with Anne and he needed to let off some steam." "Donna you're being irrational and not making any sense, no woman deserves to be beaten by anyone, I do not care how frustrated he is, Donna that does not give him the right to put his hands on you." I told Donna, "revenge is the best dish served cold and the next time that he beats you, wait until he goes to sleep. Get an extension cord, split it down to the wires, tie it to his toes, pour some cold water on his foot; this will wake him up, and when Paul realizes that you are about to electrocute him, this is when you tell him that you have taken your last beating from him. He will leave you alone. Now he is afraid of you." I saw that Donna was getting pissed off at me. She stood to leave, looked back at me. "Angelica I can not do that to a man that I love, in time he will stop. Please don't tell Paul that I've been here, he felt that I would tell you what was going on." Out of amazement, "Donna how long has this been going on?' Walking out of the door, she said, "from day one." Talking to no one, I thought, Paul is going to love her to death or she just might get a backbone and kill him or leave him. I could not resist the temptation of picking up the telephone and calling Paul, the phone rung several times before the voice mail picked up. **Hello you have reached the voice mail of the Moore and Daniels resident. We are unable to take your call at this moment. Please leave a message and we well return your call as soon as possible.** Just my luck Paul was not at home, so I decided not to leave a message.

Carlos entered the house like a mad man, stormed past me went into the kitchen. To my surprise, he came out of the kitchen with a steak knife. "Hold on little boy and where do you think that you are going with that knife?" Carlos was mad as mad could be, grabbing him by his arm. "Mommy let me go; I am going to kill that little boy down the street, teasing me about my grandmother being a drunk." I sat Carlos down next to me, "yes Carlos your grandmother likes to drink a lot and some people consider that as being a drunk, so don't let the words that people say about you or anybody else hurt your feelings. Now take that knife back into the kitchen." Doing as he was told to do, Carlos went upstairs and went to sleep. I believe my kids are from another lifetime, by the things that they say and do.

My brother Damon, may God rest his soul, twenty-six years old, and a business person owning his own towing services with a fleet of nine trucks. Damon died over bullshit. He was a people person, willing to help anyone that he came in contact with, if you needed anything Damon was there and of course most people took advantage of that.

One Saturday night Damon called me, "hey you what's up, some friends and I are going out tonight and I was wondering if you wanted to go?" Since we've been adults, not one of my brothers had ever called me to ask me to go out with them. They say it cramps there style. "Hell yea Damon I would love to go out tonight," with excitement in my voice. "Damon let me call you back on your cell phone to see if I can get a babysitter." Before I could let him get another word in edge wise, I hung up on him.

I tracked down Kelly, my girlfriend that lives down the street. She sounded as if she was asleep when she answered the phone. "Hello Angelica and how are you?" "I'm good Kelly and how are you and are you busy?" "No Angelica, what's up?"

"Damon called me and asked me to go out with him and some of his friends. If you weren't busy and if this is not too short of a notice, could you watch the kids for me?" With excitement in her voice, "of course I will Angelica; I'll be down there in a few minutes."

I called Damon on his cell phone, answering on one ring, "Angelica I will be there to pick you up around 10:00." Damon knew me all to well; I did not respond I just hung up. Good this will give me time to prepare dinner, feed the kids and give them a bath. I cooked fried chicken wings, sweet peas and mashed potatoes. By the time Kelly arrived, I feed and bathed the kids. I heard a knock on the door, "come on in Kelly." I yelled from the kitchen. She is truly a sweet heart, she moved down the street when she was about eleven years old and always hung around me, so I took her on as a sister. Kelly had very low self-esteem. Yes I will admit she is a little overweight but she has a heart of gold the size of Texas and had a very pretty face. She once told me that no man would ever want her, this made me mad and I felt sorry for her. I said, "listen Kelly if you threw a dog two bones, one with meat and one without, which one will he run to first?" She answered the one with the meat. "Well Kelly I rest my case, there are plenty of men who like thick women."

Kelly followed me into the bathroom as I flat ironed my hair. "Kelly when can you hook me up with a perm, I need one so desperately?" Running her fingers through my hair, "yes you do, I can do your hair tomorrow and of course no charge." Kelly and I are both licensed beauticians. Whenever I wanted a quick weave ponytail, she was my girl, and whenever she wants a short cut and color, I am the one she calls.

She allowed me to get dressed while she put the kids to bed. I decided to put on a red two-piece pants suit, with my red and gold heels. Checking myself out in the mirror, I don't look bad for my age plus a mother of three kids, only two years apart in age. My body is tight; I stand 5'3 and weigh 115 pounds with small tit's the size of peaches and a small butt a tight round ass, the size of a honeydew melon, smooth brown skin like chocolate ice cream, and had curves in all the right places.

Kelly walked in the room, "Angelica you look so nice." "Well thank you Miss Kelly." I heard Damon blowing the car horn; Kelly walked me to the door. "Where are you guys going tonight?" Now that was a good question, Damon did not tell me where we were going." Promising that I would tell her all about the night. We gave each other a hug. "Tell your fine ass brother I said hello." "Will do Kelly, see you later." Damon was driving his black Hummer. Sitting in the back seat was Darren, Peewee, and Peanut.

Damon was dressed to the nine, wearing a two-piece burgundy suit with a burgundy and gold tie, with his burgundy and gold gators. I loved to see my brothers dressed up, they looked so handsome. We said our hellos; I had to pull down the sun visor to look into the mirror just to get a good look at Darren's fine ass.

The three of them are childhood friends; however, Darren and Damon worked together, why the other two are around beats the hell out of me. I kept thinking about how good Darren was looking. Damon did not like the fact that his friend was digging on his sister. They made a code years ago that no friend could date a family member, that way the friendship would not be destroyed.

My mind was racing back and forth from Darren to Kelly, and whom I could hook her up with, and a way for Darren and myself to see one another with out Damon finding out. Neither one of us needed to be alone, we both deserved some happiness. I didn't hear Damon talking to me, he tapped me on my shoulder. "You look real nice." "Thank you and so do you; I see that you have on your "big boys," your gators." "You know how I do it Angelica, when I go out, I dress to impress. You never know who you might meet, maybe some potential customers." That's my brother always thinking about business. Damon just kept on driving giving me the prettiest smile. I love to see him smile; he had the kind of smile that could light up the sky, like walking on a sandy beach under the moon and the stars, with the one you love.

Peewee interrupted and said, "Angelica who's babying sitting the kids?" "Kelly and by the way Damon she told me to tell you hello." All of a sudden I hear Peewee and peanut sing the childhood song, "Kelly and Damon sitting in the tree," before the next verse came out of their mouths, Darren interjected, "shut the fuck up before I throw you out of this truck and it isn't even mine." They must have forgotten that Darren and Kelly are cousins.

We arrived to our destination, the "Hot Spot," this new club on W. Seven Mile. All the big fellas came on the weekend. The club appeared to be jumping, it was crowded. We walked in and the first person we see is Brenda. She was the neighborhood's slut. Will do anything for a dollar. Hell she even messed around with Mr. Smith's old ass. She latched on to Damon's arm and off to the dance floor they went. I couldn't tell in what direction they went dancing. Knowing what kind of person she was, this was something I didn't want to see. Peewee and Peanut were off to the bar, therefore that left me and Darren to fend for ourselves and to find an empty table. Finally finding a table we sat down, neither one of us knew what to say trying to make conversation, a sigh of relief when a high school friend walked up named Pam. "Hey Angelica and Darren, I will be your waitress for the night." After catching up on old times she took our drink order.

Me not being the drinker "Pam what liquors go into a straight fuck?" "A lot of shit, all white liquors, Gin, Vodka, Rum, Tequila, Triple Sec and splash of Papaya Juice." "Damn Pam that's a lot of shit, I think I better stick with a wine cooler and it does not matter what kind." Darren ordered himself a beer. She told us that she would be back in a few minutes with our drinks. Pam was cool, had a hard life though, her mother died when she was ten years old. By the time she was sixteen she was emancipated by the courts. Living on her own, she finished high school. She has a couple of kids now, works part time at the bar and goes to school full time to get her degree in nursing.

The silence between Darren and me was nerve wrecking. He noticed the look on my face. "Angelica what's wrong?" "Just thinking about all that liquor that was in that drink and thinking about Anne." "How long has it been since you've seen her?" I had to think for a minute. Moving his chair closer to mine. "About a year now." "Wow that is a long time. Well she chose to walk off with some man and never looked back. So don't you worry about it." Pam returned with our drinks, I took a sip of my wine cooler and it tasted good.

The dj started to play a slow song. Darren grabbed my hand, "may I have his dance?" As I stood I became light headed I guess it came from the wine cooler. I am not a drinker, Anne drunk enough for the both of us. Here comes Damon, Brenda, Peewee, his girlfriend Tonya, Peanut and his girlfriend Cynthia. As we begin to dance Darren held me so close and tight I thought that our heartbeats would become one. It seemed as if all eyes were on us. I felt like we were the only two people in the world.

As we walked, back to our table Darren had ordered drinks for all of us. Having a good time laughing and talking until the neighborhood want-a-be playboy, Pretty Tony walked by and stepped on Damon's gator shoes. That's when all hell busted wide open, Damon looked at his shoes. "Hey PT watch where you are walking man, I work hard for these shoes, and you just stepped on them and you didn't say excuse me." Looking at Tony he reminds you of an actor from the seventy's, long straight permed hair, mustache with the goatee. He stopped in mid stride turned around and looked at Damon. "Punk I don't have to say a mother fucking word, I'm pretty Tony." Damon being the hot head as he is, just waved his hand, "if you say so, I don't know about you being pretty but your name is Tony." I could feel that things were getting a little heated, and this made me feel uneasy. One of Tony's kiss ass friends Butch walked up. Slapping Tony on the back, "is there a problem PT?" "Naw man this bitch ass nigga, Damon crying about me stepping on his fake ass gators." Tony was now being sarcastic "son when you start buying your clothes at the upscale stores, spending thousands then you can say something." Damon never missed a beat giving him word for word, looked at him "want to be drug dealer and rapper. Can't sell drugs and use your own product, and as for rapping, my twin nephews can rap better then you." As Tony was walking away, he heard what Damon had said. Stepping back Tony leaned over the table "you're lucky that your fine ass sister is sitting here. If she wasn't, I would kick your ass." Hot headed Damon jumped up. "We can pretend that she is not here and take this outside." Tony knew that if he went outside by himself, he didn't stand a chance of fighting Damon. Tony was not a fighter; he stood behind his so-called boys. This was really going too far, speaking up, "Damon calm the fuck down." Damon usually listened to what I had to say. However, this time he was too mad. Butch repeated what I had just said. I turned and shot him a look that could and would kill. I calmed myself down, "Butch I don't need for you to repeat what I said." I'm quite sure that Damon heard me." Trying to keep the peace, I grabbed Tony by the hand and lead him away from everybody so they could not hear what I was saying. "Enough of this shit Tony, what is it going to take to squash this? Had the shoe been on the other foot you would have had your so called boys jump him." Tony being the ass hole that he is "Angelica the only thing that can, as you say squash this is a piece of ass." He had to be high off his own shit, I thought about it for a minute laughing in his face." Wrong answer, Tony you don't have enough money for this pussy, let alone a big enough dick, from what the girls in the hood say, you can't fuck or eat pussy, and you want some of this ass; when pigs fly. So just squash this shit, and you call yourself a playboy now that's a joke." Once he picked his face up off the floor, I didn't know Butch had heard everything that was said. Patting Tony on the back "come on PT let's go, don't waste your time on that baby making bitch." They both starting laughing, Tony laughing the loudest. "Man you're right about that bitch; she will never lay a baby on me, PT a baby's daddy, now that's some funny shit." Before Tony and Butch walked off, I walked back to them. "If you two are going to call me a bitch give me my respect and call me "MISS BITCH," if I'm one, then what does that make your mothers?" Then I walked back to the table. Not looking back to see if they were still standing there. The guys did not hear what was said but Brenda's ass did. I know her all to well; she could not wait to get back to the block to tell people what had happen. She will hang around Tony and his crew and listen to what they had to say and then try to hang around Damon to win some brownie points with him. Lord knows this bitch couldn't keep her mouth shut.

This had spoiled everyone's mood, we decided to leave. Brenda did not want Damon to leave, "Damon don't go, stay a little while longer. We were having fun don't let PT get to you, so come on and stay." Damon stood up "Brenda I know where you are going with this, sorry but my answer is no, we will always be friends, nothing else." We left Brenda sitting there with her mouth wide open. "Fuck you Damon, you're not a man anyway, you can't handle this." That's all we heard as Damon paid everyone's tab as we were walking out of the door.

Peewee and Peanut said their good byes to their girl friends. The ride on the way home was quiet. Darren was the one who broke the ice, "Damon don't let that shit with Tony sweat or stress you out man. You know that he was just trying to show off in front of his friends." Damon did not respond, I could feel that something was not right with him. Therefore, I left it alone; I knew that when he wanted to talk to me about it, he would. I changed the subject, "did you see the look on Brenda's face when Damon turned her down for the millionth time?" That gave us a good laugh, the laugh in Peewee's and Peanut's voice let it be known that they were scared of PT.

We dropped the two scary cats off then Damon pulled into Darren's driveway. He walked around to the driver's side; doing the manly thing, they bumped fists. Then he came around to my side of the car, kissing me on my hand, "good night Miss Angelica thank you for the dance. With a lost for words, I just smiled. Damon backed out of the driveway "what was that all about?" Giving him a childish look, "now Damon that was nothing and you don't have to say anything I know the code." No friend of yours can date a family member."

As we parked in front of my house. We sat there in total silence. "What wrong Damon, I know that you are not worried about that nigga?" "No way girl but there is one thing that I need to talk to you about." I turned around in the seat, he had my undivided attention. "Angelica I am ready to settle down and be in a serious relationship." Me being me, "with who Brenda?" If looks could kill, I would have been a goner, "no stupid, if I hook up with that hoe I would have the alphabet disease, she would give me everything from A to Z." I laughed so hard I thought that I was going to pee on myself.

A look of calm and peace came over Darren, "I've liked Kelly for sometime now, and I know about the code we made. I was in total shock, "ok Damon, for real, if this is true and if you feel this way. Treat her right don't lead her on, she deserves happiness and if this makes you happy then I'm all for it. It's so late; will you drop her off at home?' Darren gave me a kiss on the forehead, "good night sis and I'll call you later when I think you're awake."

I walked into the house; Kelly was watching T.V. "Angelica, all is well, the kids are fast asleep." "Thank you Kelly for watching them for me, you are a life saver." Walking her to the door. "Damon is going to drop you off and I promise that I will tell you all about our night out." I locked the door jumped in the shower and got into bed. I could not stop thinking about Darren, before I knew it, my hands were in between my legs and I started masturbating. It was not what I wanted but it will do for now. For the life of me, I don't know why I don't have any adult toys hidden some where in my bedroom.

Chapter 2

Today is going to be another scorcher; the kids are with there Uncle Paul. It has been a month since our outing to the club.   While sitting on the front porch enjoying a tall cold glass of lemonade, I saw Mrs. Peterson hose her porch down with water from where the kids had spilled pop and candy; not wanting to attract bugs, "Good morning Mrs. Peterson." She looked around and waved her hand.

I was not ready for his shit; here comes my brother Melvin, who wants to be a pimp. He refuse to get a job, he's living with a female dancer named Hair. Her real name is Monique; she dances at some club called Cupcakes. She's light brown skinned and has tits the size of a small head of cabbage. Her body is shaped like a pop bottle. With her long jet black hair, let

Melvin tell it, she's the first pony in his stable. What that girl will do and give him, I will never understand. Walking up on the front porch, here he comes. "What's up Mel?' Giving me a hug and a kiss, "just chilling, where are my niece and nephews?" "They are with Paul." Melvin not biting his tongue when it comes to words, "you mean to tell me his mean ass did something for somebody like watch your kids? Hell I called him, he didn't even give me a chance to say anything, he barked in my ear, whatever it is you want I'm not going to give it to you. Then he hung up on me." "Don't sound so surprised Mel, you're not the only one who doesn't come and get your niece and nephews and further more you need to GET A JOB, so you can stop asking people for shit " "I have a job, me, "Mel the PIMP," love the kids to death but no can do."

Saved by his cell phone ringing. "Oh shit! This is Shannon calling me; right now I don't feel like hearing her bitch about this and that. I'll let her leave me a voice mail message." That is my sister and whenever I hear her name, it makes my skin crawl. "Mel when you do talk to her, tell Miss Shannon she could return my phone calls sometimes." "That's just it," Mel exclaimed, "I'm so tired of hearing about the argument the two of you had." Giving me a pat on my head and a kiss on my cheek, "when I do talk to her I will tell her to call you." Oh here, give this to my niece and nephews." Handing me three ten dollar bills before he walked off the porch. "Thanks" is all I could say before he started the car and pulled off.

Oh, I forgot about the other two dancers that Melvin hangs out with. Now there is Peaches, her real name is Serena, dark as the night with hazel brown eyes, short in height; 4'7 with curly hair, smooth black skin, full lips and a gap between her teeth that's sexy as hell. Her measurements are 38, 24, and 36. A waist that would make a fat woman jealous and an ass that would make a grown man sob. Moreover, the sad thing is, she is gay, as gay is gay. If I liked licking splits, I would holler at her in a heartbeat. Then there is Sapphire real name is Sophia, a pure red bone, 5'8 in height, pencil thin and small tit's the size of plums. Thin lips and shoulder length sandy brown hair. She reminds you of your favorite bank teller or your child's second grade teacher. To see her outside the club you would never believe that she was a dancer. I give credit where it's due; she works hard for her money. She's going to college, studying Criminal Justice. Mel's broke ass thinks he's the shit.

My head began to itch; I wish I could find Kelly; this ponytail is driving me crazy. She needs to come and hook a sister up. Well speak of the devil; hear she comes now, "hey Kelly haven't seen you in a while." Blushing she said, "Damon and I have been spending a lot of time together." "Kelly you look so happy," I replied. "Angel I am, I've never felt like this before, I think I'm dreaming and I never want to wake up." By this time, I am getting hungry. "Kelly you want something to eat?" "What ever you're having is fine with me." I grabbed my glass and went into the kitchen, "Kelly do you think you can do my hair tomorrow if Sir Damon does not have you all day?" I hear her laughing, "of course I can, I will make the time and as you call him, Sir Damon will have to wait." I come back outside with cut up apples, cheese, assorted crackers and bottle water. Kelly looked at my hair, "yes most definitely I will do your hair, it looks jacked up." We both begin to laugh, then out in a close distant we hear gunshots. "This neighborhood is getting worse and worse Kelly; I was thinking it's time to move, I have three kids to think about." "Yea Angelica, I was thinking the same thing. We've been on this street all of our lives." Then there was a second set of gunshots. All of a sudden, Kelly dropped her water bottle. "Angelica something is not right I have a feeling that somebody is hurt and hurt bad." We see people running down the street. "Come on Angelica let's go down to the corner and see what is going on." I picked up my keys, cell phone, closed the door, and down the street, we went.

We decided to walk, while walking, police cars flew pass with siren's blaring, and as we reached the corner, my heart dropped to my shoes, I could not believe my eyes, there was my brother Damon laying face down in a pool of blood. Kelly let out a scream that sounded like it came from the depths of her soul. Lying next to Damon was Jasmine, Tony's girlfriend, the only one that would put up with his shit. Across from her was a friend of ours name Kevin and they all appeared to be hurt badly.

I just stood there in total shock unable to move. The police were talking to Darren. The EMS shouted, "Let's go I have a pulse on this one." Talking about Damon, the police said that we could follow them to the hospital. We followed the police and rode in silence never saying one word to each other. I called my sisters and brothers. Kelly called our friends, I heard her say that we were going to Heavenly Hospital.

We arrived at the hospital and a nurse put us in a private waiting room. A few minutes later the police walked in and sat down, "ok Darren let's start from the beginning." Darren was talking to the police officer; I think his name was Officer Brown. "Back to the night at the Hot Spot." Officer Brown interrupted and said, "I hate that damn club." In walk Shannon, Paul, Andrea, Tom, and Melvin frantic. Shannon walk's over and gives me a hug.

Darren went on to explain, "We were playing basketball on the corner of San Juan. Tony and his boys drove by and shot off a round of bullets. When we heard the first set of gun shots, we just stood there. The only thing that was said was that he needs to grow up and with all these kids around, somebody can get hurt. We went back to playing ball, all of a sudden we heard tires screeching, they pulled up into the lot and starting shooting again. People started running trying to find cover. That's when I saw Damon, Jasmine, and Kevin fall to the ground."

Finally the doctor came in and whispered something into Officer Brown's ear. He excused himself. Before the doctor, could leave I stood up "doctor how is our brother?" "Sorry Miss I am not the doctor that is working on your brother.

I am working on the other two that were shot, Kevin and Jasmine." Shannon stood beside me "how are they doing?" The doctor replied, "Kevin will never walk again, and the Parkers will be burying there daughter, I'm sorry but I have to go now." Another doctor came into the room with Officer Brown and introduced himself "I'm Dr. Jefferson; there is no easy way for me to tell you this, my staff and I did all that we could do for Damon, there was so much blood loss due to him being shot six times. I am truly sorry for your lost; please take as much time as you need in here and if there is any thing you need just push that button on the wall."

I must have fainted, I remember Darren and Paul picking me up and laying me on the couch. Hearing a knock on the door, were Kevin and Jasmine's parents. Hugging us all and giving there condolence, and we all did like wise. Mrs. Parker turned around and declared, "REMMBER GOD MAKES NO MISTAKES."I regained my composure "Officer Brown I want you to find and arrest number one -Anthony Cunningham aka Pretty Tony, and number two - Sylvester Beach aka Butch."

Officer Brown pulled out his notebook, "does anyone know where these two live?" Darren excused himself to make a few telephone calls, to find out the two addresses the officer demanded, a few minutes later, "Tony lives at 17849 Lynise Dr., and Butch lives at 13841 Lynette Ave." Officer Brown extended his hand, "please believe me Moore family, I am going to do everything in my power to arrest these two people." Paul walked the officer to the door. This is unreal; I sat there in a daze with what appeared to be tears falling down my face. Paul walked back in, "you won't believe whose out in the hallway." My eyes grew big as car tires. He must have seen the fear in my face. "It's no one but our drunken ass mother Anne." I'm thinking what in the hell was she doing here. Sashaying her drunken ass in the room, what I saw was the nightmare from hell.

Anne looked like a walking corpse, hair all matted together, and a body order that could choke a goat. She smelled like rotten garbage. This pissed Shannon off "Anne what in the fuck are you doing here, we have not seen you in months?" Anne was good and drunk her words slurred and we could barely understand what she was saying, "I just lost my son, what the fuck do you mean what I am doing here?"

Well all begin to look around to see who had called her. Andrea dropped her head, my temperature begin to rise. "Andrea I will deal with you later." Shannon and I decided to go out into the hallway because the smell of Anne was getting on our nerves. By the time we reached the door, I guess the smell of Anne was bothering Melvin "Anne, momma or whatever in the hell your name is today, sit the hell down, you smell bad."

Once in the hallway we could breathe a breath of fresh air. Looking at Shannon, "this is all we need Anne being here looking foul and a hot mess." Shannon broke down leaning into my shoulder crying so hard I thought that she was going to stop breathing. "Angelica I feel like I played a part into Damon dying." "Shannon what in the hell are you talking about?" I replied. We sat down in some chairs that were in the hallway. "Angelica, Damon called me the night you all went out, being the bitch that I am, I told him that I did not want to go with his fake ass friends to some damn club in the ghetto." Shannon was right, she's a bitch, "Shannon you being there would not have made a difference, and the same shit would have happen." "No Angelica, I feel like Tony would not have said anything to Damon." Not following, she continued, "Angelica I never told anyone this so keep this to yourself, I was still fucking around with Tony for the first two years of me and Michael's relationship." Now my mouth hit the floor, no words could come out.

The nurse walked up, so we changed the conversation, "Angelica where are the kids?" said Shannon. That was a good question. "Knowing Paul, either Donna is watching them or they are over to Mrs. Peterson's house. As we signed all the paper work, Shannon said, "good Angelica they don't need to see and be around all of this especially seeing Anne like she is." As we walked back to the room Shannon and I both agreed that the first thing we should do first is call Pips Funeral Home to come and pick up our brothers remains and that we should do that as soon as we get to my house.

Thoughts of my brother's dead body and all that blood made me feel sick, but I still could gather enough emotional strength to think back on how my brother lived his life, this was a waste I thought, how anyone could do this to him was mind boggling. I hope they fry the bastards that did this.

I knew I had to be strong for myself and my brothers and sisters. As exasperated as I was, I knew it was going to tough for all of us, even Anne.

Entering the room to my surprise, everyone was quiet. However, the smell of Anne killed you.

We all rode home in silence. We pulled up in front of the house; the news had spread fast about Damon being dead. There were people everywhere. Shannon and I took Anne to the side, "you need to go wherever you live and take a bath before you come back and if you choose not to come back that's fine with me," Barked Shannon. Anne did not try to defend herself she walked off.

I walked into the house and there is Shannon ranting and raving. "I can't believe this shit; our brother was killed over Tony stepping on his shoes." I interrupted her ranting and raving. "Shannon hold on, Brenda's mouth played a part in all of this as well." The sound of Brenda's name made Shannon's face turn with displeasure. Before Shannon couldn't say a word, Melvin beat her to the punch. "What did that bitch have to do with this?" "You see as soon as we walked into the club, Brenda's ass hung onto Damon like she was his third arm."

I begin to lose my voice from all the crying that I had done, I managed to say "no disrespect Kelly." Then once again, I begin to cry. Kelly came to me and hugged me, "none taken sweetie,

43

he told me everything." Therefore, Darren took where I left off. I went back into my daze, the last thing I heard Darren say, "You see, Brenda saw and heard everything. So there is no telling what she said when we left." Shannon was heated, grabbed her purse "If I find out that slut had anything to do with this, I am going to whip her ass and no one and I mean no one is going to stop me." I heard her close my bedroom door. Kelly just sat there sobbing crying so hard that Mel went and set beside her and tried to console her. She gave him a half a smile "Mel you're alright, considering what others may think of you," poking him in his side. "I'm just kidding with you, thank you." That made us laugh a little.

Shannon came out of my bedroom wearing a pair of my blue jeans shorts, a tee shirt, and a pair of my socks. "Angelica I hope that you do not mind I borrowed some of your clothes. I had to get out of those work clothes." Giving her a smile, I just waved my hand to let her know it was ok. Friends began to come into the house. Shannon, Kelly and I went into the kitchen to prepare some food just in case someone was hungry.

I had almost forgotten, I picked up the phone and called Pips Funeral Home. A very squeaky voice, "thank you for calling Pips Funeral Home;

this is Gloria how may I help you?" "Gloria my name is Angelica Moore; I am calling to release my brother's body to your funeral home." "Ms. Moore what is the decease's name?" "Damon Moore and he's at Heavenly Hospital." "One more question, is there a phone number where I can reach the family when his body comes in?" "555-5511." "Thank you Ms. Moore we will give you a call and I am truly sorry for your loss." "Thank you so much, Good bye."

Shannon, Kelly and I sat down to smoke a cigarette trying to calm ourselves down. "Angelica, Kelly and I are going to kick Brenda's ass as soon as we see her," Shannon exclaimed. All of a sudden we hear all this commotion; we rush to see what was going on in the living room. With everything that had been going on, we didn't notice that Andrea and Tom had left and returned. Anne was drunker then drunk pushing Andrea around, "you crack head hoe." Thank goodness that the only people that were here were just family and friends. Who were use to the Moore family drama.

Everyone's nerves were frazzled; Kelly could not take it anymore, "just stop it." We all looked at her in surprise. "Damon my one and only true love is dead. Anne just look at you, you should be ashamed of yourself. You're drunk and smell awful. Andrea you are so high you don't know if you are coming or going. Do either of you care that Damon is dead?" Anne did a 360 degree turn, "who in the hell do you think you're talking to in my house?" Kelly stood and approaches Anne, "the last time I checked this was Angelica Denise Moore's house." It took Anne a minute to think of something to say, "even though I'm not around, I know things. I know that you're nothing but a plaything to Damon." Kelly went into her purse and pulled out an envelope, opened the papers up and turned them around for all to see. "Anne, as for who in the hell I think I am, according to these papers the last time I checked I AM MRS. DAMON MARCEL MOORE, that's who in the hell I know am." All of our mouths hit the floor. Paul looked at the papers "yes sir she is Damon's wife alright. It seems as if they were married two weeks ago today." Tears begin to stream down my face, "Kelly why didn't you tell any of us?" Coming to sit beside me rubbing me on the back of my hands. "Angelica, Damon and I were planning a surprise dinner this coming Saturday to announce that we were married."

Kelly by this time was weeping; looking into her purse she pulled out her wedding rings kissed them and put them on her finger. Shannon went to console her. Oh, this broke my heart. We all stared at Anne looking like an old broke down car. Anne must have had enough time to think of something to say. "Well Kelly you might be his wife on paper, but you are not my daughter in-law, my true daughter in-law should have been Brenda, which was his true love." Kelly knew better she didn't respond to what Anne had said.

Anne was unbelievable; this is what she wanted to do, cause a problem between us. That's how she was. Looking at Mel, "boy go get me a pint of whiskey." Paul cut in, "Mel you are not going anywhere, if that drunk wants to drink, let her walk her ass to the store and get it herself and if she does, she can keep on walking." Anne stood up fixed her clothes, face to face, Paul and she stood, "Paul who do you think you are? I am your mother and you are not Mel's mother?" "You were never a mother to any of us, Paul replied. You were a piece of ass to any man who would buy you whiskey and cigarettes."

I could see that things were getting out of hand, I had had enough. "Anne sit down and be quiet, and if you can't, you can leave." Andrea was pacing "Andrea if you need a fix you can get out as well. Look at the way you all are acting."

Damon would not want this, Damon is dead, and we don't need this shit from the two of you." They sat there and did not say a word. "I mean it, one more word out of the two of you, I will throw your asses out and you will never step foot in this house again. Do I make myself clear?"

Tiredness and me being mad had set in, I begun to shake, Paul came to me, "Angelica go and lay down for awhile we can handle things here." I did just that, by the time I laid down I heard the doorbell ring. That's when the shouting begun, I jumped up ran to the living room and who do I see, Brenda's ass. Paul is holding Shannon; I knew that he would let her go at any given moment. Therefore, I stood in between the three of them. "Brenda what are you doing here?" "Angelica you know that I had to come by, you know that I loved me some Damon?"

Paul still holding Shannon and she was as red as red could be, "bitch he didn't love you back, that's some fantasy that you made up in that sick head of yours, and by the way Brenda do you know Kelly?" Brenda looked at Kelly and rolled her eyes. "Well bitch she is Damon's wife, they were married two weeks ago." Brenda's mouth hit the floor. "Paul let me go," yells Shannon, "I am not going to hit this embarrassed hoe."

Shannon calmed down. "Brenda you're the reason why Damon is dead." Brenda began to stumble over her words, "what are you talking about Shannon?" Shannon gave Brenda a wicked laugh "I have made telephone calls, and all I heard was Brenda said this Brenda said that. You were at the club the night that shit went down with Damon and Tony; you were hanging onto my brother like a wet swim suit." Brenda cut her eyes over to Kelly; Kelly walked over and put her hand on Shannon's shoulder, "Kelly bet you didn't know that." As a matter of fact, yes I did sweetie," Kelly said in a sarcastic tone. "He told me everything, how you offered to take him home with you. He turned you down by telling you that the two of you will always be friends but nothing more. He left your ass sitting there at the table. It was not his style to turn around to see what you were doing. He knew you all to well, knowing that you would haul your ass off to be with Tony and his boys." Brenda could not get a word in. Kelly continued, "Tony didn't want you there with him and his boys. We all know that Tony has a fetish and let it be known. He knew you would suck his dick, and that you liked to be fucked in the ass like a dog, and when he's done with you, he throws you to one of his boys."

"Now, you see Brenda, my husband and when I say my husband, he told me everything. I even know that the two of you use to be a couple a few years ago." We all looked at Kelly, we were shelled shocked. Brenda got ready to say something and in a blink of an eye, Shannon jumped up and hit Brenda so hard that blood flew across the room. Melvin grabbed Shannon, "Brenda you need to leave, I don't know how much longer I can hold Shannon; she is gutting to get you." Shannon yells, "Brenda revenge is the best dish served cold, so one day, a week, a month, or a year, I am going to get you, so you better watch your back."

By this time, Andrea and Tom needed a fix from the crack pipe. Anne needed to drink her dinner, so they left without saying a word, they've seen enough drama. All I could say was 'thank god." As they were leaving Mrs. Peterson, was knocking on the door bringing the kids home. She hugged me so tight, "if there is anything that my family can do for you Angelica just come over or call." As she was leaving, she begins to cry, so Melvin helped her across the street. Cedric climbed up into Shannon's lap, "Aunt Shannon why is Mrs. Peterson crying?" This broke all of your hearts. Shannon hugged Cedric, "there is something that

I need to tell you, come here Carlos and Denise. Something terrible has happen."

Denise being inquisitive, "Aunt Shannon I know about Uncle Damon already, but my brothers don't." This was getting the best of Cedric and Carlos, there was something that she knew, and they did not. Shannon hugged the boys and looked them in there eyes. "Your Uncle Damon has died, do you understand what that means." They both shook there heads, yes. Carlos being the more talkative one, "will he go to heaven like my gold fish skip?" "Yes, sweetie he will go to heaven like skip," Shannon explained. She kissed him on his forehead, he jumped down and off to the kitchen the children went, they have stomachs like a bottomless pit.

Paul went into the den, "Angelica come here." I walked into the den, he was on the phone. "I just called Donna and we're going to take the kids for you. You need to get some rest, so Donna just ordered some pizza and I am going to rent some movies. Don't worry about packing there clothes, they have some at the house." We hugged and sat in silence for a few minutes. Back in the living room I sat down, "kids come here, Uncle Paul is going to take you home with him tonight, I want you to behave yourselves, if not Uncle Paul is going to whip you." Knowing Paul would never whip them. We said our good nights; I knew they would be back early in the morning. Friends came and went, there was no one left but Kelly and myself. She locked the door after saying her good byes to Shannon, "Angelica do you mind if I spend the night with you?" I told her of course not, because in the back of my mind I didn't want to be alone.

Kelly sat down next to me as I was lighting a cigarette. "Angelica I am so sorry for yelling at Anne, I just snapped. I couldn't take it anymore; all of this is too much for me." "Kelly what is there to be sorry for? In addition, you don't have to explain anything to me, you're family now." You could see the look in her eyes that she truly loved Damon. "Angelica I wanted to tell you so bad that Damon and I were married, but I made a promise to him that we would tell everyone at the same time."

She had taken me back to the night we all went out and Damon dropped her off. "He had parked the car and we talked for hours, things like, what he wanted to do in the future. He then told me how much he like me, for how long and you know there was no secret that I liked him. The only reason he didn't say anything to me was because of some damn code he and Darren had taken up about dating family, which I think is stupid. We talked so long that the sun was coming up. We exchanged telephone numbers; we said our goodnight and good mornings as he walked me to the door. He then leaned over and kissed me on my cheek; it was so soft like rubbing a rose petal on your skin. Angelica that whole morning I was thinking that it might have been the liquor talking and that no one like Damon could ever like someone like me. While cooking breakfast that morning the doorbell rung, there was a delivery man wanting to know if I were a Kelly Andrews? I told him that I was she, he handed me a box with two dozen long stem roses."

I excused myself and went to the bathroom, coming out I grabbed a notebook and pen. I knew that when we finished this conversation we would have to get his obituary together. I came back into the living room. "Ok Kelly where were you?" "Darren had set down to breakfast; he noticed the roses and asked me where did they come from." "Damon," I said. "I explained to Darren about the conversation that Damon and I had. Darren told me to stop, that I didn't need to explain anything else to him. Darren asked if I liked Damon, I told him yes, for years. I guess the gleam in my eyes told it all. We would spend every available moment we could together. One night he picked me up and took me over to his house. As we entered his house he had candles lit throughout the house, soft music playing in the background. Handing me a glass of wine, he told me to sit down and relax while he prepared dinner. He cooked lobster, shrimp, tossed green salad and for dessert strawberry cheese cake. After dinner he led me into the living room, sat me down on the couch and gave me a foot massage. Damon then excused himself, a few minutes later he came back with this big ass teddy bear. Handing me the bear, girl I was all smiles, I sat the bear on the floor next to me. When I looked up there was Damon down on one knee, saying that he wanted me to make him the happiest man alive. Would I become Mrs. Damon Marcel Moore? With tears streaming down my face, I looked at Damon and said, out of all the women he could have, why me? I am not supermodel material, I am overweight, before I could say another word he told me to stop that, and why not me? I have the personality, the brains and furthermore there are a lot of brothers out here that like a plus size woman. Angelica I said yes and two days later we went downtown and like that we were married, Darren was our witness. Now what gets me, he applied for the license the day he sent me the roses, he just knew that I was going to say yes."

Kelly had me in tears, that was so romantic. Kelly picked up one of my cigarettes, lit it and took a long drag off of it. "Angelica this is what scares me, Damon told me he felt that Tony was going to get him for trying to embarrass him at the club. I told Damon to stop the nonsense, Tony was not crazy and there were too many eyewitnesses as to what happen that night. I guess I was wrong."

Kelly and I decided to start on the obituary, looking through photos we could not find any that were appropriate so we decided no pictures, Kelly thought that we should bury him in the suit that he wore to the club that night. The sun began to peek through the mini blinds. It was time for us to get some shuteye, between yawns I said, "Kelly we have a long day in head of us, there's one question I need to ask, how do we get through this?" Hugging me, "Angelica one day at a time, I am a firm believer that God does not put any more on us then we can bear." On that note, we went to bed.

Chapter 3

I awaken to the smell of bacon cooking, so I just laid there in my own thoughts praying that Damon's death was just a dream. Then I heard Shannon's big ass mouth, I knew I wasn't dreaming. My family knew I was tired and I guess they wanted me to sleep in. Looking at the clock on the wall, it was already 10:00am. I hear a light knock on my bedroom door, pretending I didn't hear it; the knock became louder. "Come in." It was only Mel "Angelica are you alright?" "Yes Mel, as well as can be expected." Mel shaking my bed, I decided that it was time for me to get up. Hearing loud talking, "Mel who in the world is out there?" "Oh just the gang, Shannon, Paul, Kelly and Darren." Just knowing that Darren was here made me feel a lot better. "Ok Mel let me get myself together and I will be out in a few minutes." I went into the bathroom washed up and put some clothes on. Walking into the kitchen the gang had grown, Peewee and Peanut were here. Kelly was busy frying bacon, scrambling eggs, sausage, and grits. Boy did that food smell good. We sat down to the table, Mel said grace, ***"Thank you Lord for this food we are about to receive, give us the strength to make it through the death of our brother, husband and friend Damon, we are asking all these blessing in Jesus name Amen."***

There was a knock at the door; Paul is not a morning person, who in the world could this be? Paul getting up to answer the door shouting, "oh nobody special, just your trick ass friends Angelica, Tammy and Carla." None of my family liked these two; they feel that Tammy and Carla were beneath me. I have to admit, they were a little trashy. Tammy being the bitch that she is. "Good the fuck morning to you to Paul and hello to the rest of the Moore family." Shoving a bag of bagels and orange juice at him. Carla handed Mel some muffins, cheese and fruit tray.

Now the telephone began to ring, I didn't know what the problem with Paul was. Snatching the receiver off the hook, "hello, hold on, this is Anthony and Mark they want to know if we need anything from the store?" Shannon yells, "smokes, what kind it doesn't matter." I had plenty of cigarettes so therefore I did not need anything. Paul continues, "Anthony did you hear loud mouth Shannon? We need some paper plates, cups, napkins and a couple bags of ice if that's not too much for you. Alright then, see you in a minute."

Looking around for my children "Paul where are my rug rats?" "Shannon saw Byron at the gas station, told him what happen, he came and picked up Denise while you were asleep. I ran into big Cedric at the carwash, he already knew, he told me to tell you, just give him an hour and he would pick the boys up. Also while you were sleep, Kelly and I took the obituary to the printers."

It was a relief to me that the kid's fathers were going to pick them up for me. In a time of crises, I knew they would come through for me. I must say that these were two good men that fathered my children, Bryon and Big Cedric. We just had personal things which circumvented our being together.

Kelly walked up behind me and put her arm around my neck, "Angelica the kids do not need to be around this so there father's agreed to keep them until the funeral was over with. They did not want the kids to have nightmares with seeing there Uncle Damon in a casket." I agreed absolutely, I could not handle the kids having nightmares. I tapped Paul on his shoulder, "come out in the backyard and have a smoke with me." Once outside I knew that I had a fight on my hands, I was getting ready to mention about him beating on Donna. After being out there for a minute, a cold chill went all through my body and I decided not to say anything. Therefore, we just stood there in silence. Breaking the ice, "you know Paul even though myself and the kid's dads could not stay together, they are alright." He did not say anything; he just shook his head in agreement and appeared to be in deep thought. Now in the back of my mind I knew that I would have to walk lightly around Paul the rest of the day, "where is Donna?" Looking at his watch, "she should be here any minute." He was admiring my outfit, "Angelica, are you going to wear that to the funeral home today?" Giving him a funny look, "oh shit don't tell me sorry ass Mel did not call you last night to tell you that we have an appointment today at 1:00 with Mr. Jones to make the arrangements."

My blood was boiling over, "no that fool did not call me." Paul and I damn near ran each other over trying to get into the house. The kitchen was clean and everyone was in the living room. Melvin was on his cell phone, so I slapped him upside his head. Whomever he was talking to, he told them he had to call them back. "Have you lost your mind Angelica?" Giving me a childish look, I got ready to hit him again, "no I have not lost my mind but you've lost yours.

Weren't you supposed to call me last night and inform me about the appointment at the funeral home today?" "Oh shit Angelica my bag, I forgot, like I told you, a pimp's work is never done," beating himself on the chest. Shannon walked by and hit him in the same spot as I did, "get yourself a real job, you ain't no pimp." Melvin was pissed off that Shannon had hit him in the same spot but he knew not to say anything to her.

Kelly was sitting on the front porch, Shannon and I went out there to keep her company. Running my fingers through her hair, "are you alright sister-in-law?" Kelly kissed her wedding rings, "yes, I'm fine; just sitting here having a private conversation with God and Damon, asking for them to give us strength to get through all this madness." Shannon let out a loud sigh, "guess whose coming?" Here comes Andrea, Tom and Anne, we all walk in the house, Shannon grabbed all of our purses, put them in my room and locked the door. Handing me my house keys, I noticed Andrea's eyes, they were as wide as a fat man's waist, who just finished eating at an all you can eat buffet.

I looked at the three of them, "I am warning you I am not taking any of your bullshit. Say one word, do one thing, I will put your asses out and you can never come back." Paul was becoming very impatient, "what time is it?" Melvin looked at the clock on his phone, "it is 11:45 and we have a long way to go." Andrea did not notice that Shannon and I were watching her, and Tom was trying to get her to sit down. She walks over, mumbles, "um, um Angelica I'm not feeling well. Can I lie across your bed?" Andrea was already making a fool out of herself, to keep from having further embarrassment on her part, Shannon and I took her into the kitchen to talk to her. "Listen Andrea, Shannon and I are no fools; we know that you need a fix. You saw Shannon take our purses into my bedroom. Now do you really think I'm going to let you go in my room and lay across my bed? If you think yes, wrong answer. We love you but I'm not going to let you steal from us." Before Andrea could say a word, Shannon put her arm around her trying to be a sister "now if you really don't feel well, you can lay on the couch in the den. Andrea you need to go into a drug treatment program." Andrea snatched Shannon's arm from around her neck, "you bitches, I don't need any damn treatment program." She stormed out of the kitchen. I looked at my watch it is only noon. This madness is really working on my nerves.

I am sitting in the chair looking out of the window, "Paul you and Melvin go help Donna and Mrs. Peterson with some of the food." As soon as Donna walked in, "Paul I am sorry for being late, when I pulled up Mrs. Peterson asked me to come and help her with this food. I didn't want to rush her." He took the food out of her hands, kissed her on the cheek. "That's ok baby, I know how slow she can be."

Oh shit I can't wait until all of this is over with; I know I sound like a broken record. I'm observing everyone's mood and conversation, Anne is asking Melvin for some money, of all people. I'm tired of her shit; I stand in the middle of the floor and start to scream. Scaring the hell out of everyone. "This is it, I'm tired and Anne get your shit and get the hell out. I warned you if you did one thing or said something out of the way, you were out of here. Why in the hell are you asking Mel for some money? Do you need a drink that damn bad that you have to ask your youngest son for some money? Just like Andrea and Tom, you need help as well. Anne please leave and do not come back, you don't know me or this house." She resented the fact that I told her to get out. Before she could say anything, I interrupted, "please Anne leave before I do something that I will regret." Anne grabbed her purse and walked out. I guess she thought about what I had said because she came back in the house, looked at me and snarled, "who in the hell do you think you are talking to me like this?" I yelled back, "I'm Angelica Denise Moore, that's who and do not forget it." By this time, I am standing there shaking and crying.

Donna comes and hugs me, "Angelica it's going to be alright, Damon wouldn't want this." "I know Donna; I'm just tired of all this mess." Paul interrupted, "it's time for us to be going to the funeral home." Donna agreed to stay with my friends who were enjoying the drama that was unfolding in front of their eyes. At this point, I didn't give a damn. Andrea and Tom stood up as if they wanted to go, but Shannon and Paul told them they couldn't go. Andrea turned beet red, "look Shannon I'm tired of you and Angelica excluding me from everything, Damon was my brother too." Kelly spoke up, "Andrea I don't know about Tom but you are high as hell and need to stay here. We can handle this." She jumped in Kelly's face, "you haven't been in this family long enough to say shit to me so just sit your fat ass down." Before I knew it, Kelly hauled off and slapped Andrea, knocking her down in the chair. Andrea looked at Kelly as if she were getting ready to say something but changed her mind. "Now Andrea my fat ass is getting ready to go and make arrangements for my husband's funeral, I advise you to stay in that chair if you know what's good for you." To my surprise, she never got up.

On the ride to the funeral home, Kelly told us that she was sorry for slapping Andrea. Shannon turned around in her seat, "Kelly stop it right now, lets get one thing straight, you don't have to apologize to us for anything. You are our sister-in-law and furthermore Andrea's ass needed it." Paul cleared his throat, "I'm not trying to change the subject, but how are we going to pay for Damon's funeral?" Kelly said "Don't worry about that, Damon had several insurance policies."

We met with Mr. Jones; the family hour is at 12:30p.m. and the funeral will be held at 1:00p. m. I was wondering how Melvin felt, our brother had been violently gunned down, I could never understand how my brothers felt because they had a special bond, I knew they were just as devastated as I was but now a piece of their bond is gone.

Melvin was the only one who did not say much of anything, finally he spoke up, "I am like Angelica we have five more days of this shit. I wonder do white people go through this."

We get back home to find that my friends had left; Tom was sitting in the chair, Donna was in the kitchen washing dishes. Looking at Tom, "where is Andrea?" he began to cry, "She left." I sat next to him, "Angelica I hate to have this monkey on my back. It's bad enough, the only source of income is my disability check and Andrea has lost her job at the post office." We all exclaimed, "Say what?" Tom continued, "there is so much that you do not know." Taking a deep breath, I said, "tell us everything. "The supervisor on her job caught her getting high in her car on lunch break. They wrote her up and made her take random drug test, which she was able to pass. The next thing she did while delivering mail; she stole someone's income tax refund check, got a fake I. D. and cashed it. After being caught, she confessed. Needless to say, she was fired and made to pay restitution. Even though she lost her job, we still were getting high, so one day I asked her where did all the money come from, all the lawsuit money was almost gone; I've seen all the bank statements. She told me not to worry." "At the time I didn't care as long as we had enough crack. So finally I got fed up and I followed her. What I saw made me sick, I could not believe my eyes, I saw Andrea in the back of the vacant store on the corner, bending over sucking Tony's dick, while Butch fucked her in her ass. Before I made this discovery I knew something was wrong, our sex life had changed dramatically, she wanted me to do things that we've never done before. When you guys left going to the funeral home, I took her out on the porch, sat her down, and told her that I was tired of getting high. I knew how and where she was getting her money from. I suggested that we get some help; she told me she didn't need any damn help, copped an attitude and stormed off to Mrs. Peterson's house. I'm for sure she asked her for some money and knowing Mrs. Peterson she couldn't tell her no." We all sat there speechless, not knowing what to say, after telling him how proud I was of him to admit that he had a problem and he wanted to get help. "Regardless if she gets high or not, I'm still going to be with her. Yes, that's my wife and I will hold onto our vows, **FOR BETTER OR FOR WORSE, FOR**

RICHER OR POORER IN SICKNESS AND IN HEALTH, TILL DEATH DO US PART. I wouldn't care if she never comes back; I just want this monkey off my back. Please forgive me for talking in riddles and raising my voice, I'm just confused and coming down off of my last high, Angelica I love Andrea and I know she needs help. I'm going to get myself together and I hope your sister follows suite, if she doesn't, I don't know what I'm going to do, I hope this doesn't end in divorce." Shannon spoke up "stop it; we'll handle this after we bury Damon, we can only handle one problem at a time."

Tom stood up and began to pace the floor, "I hate the fact that I got hooked on crack cocaine, I saw what it had done to other people and I've even looked down on them. Now look at me, I know someone is frowning and looking down on me now. Once again, can you ever forgive me?" Paul walked over to him, "hey, no one put a gun to your head and made you smoke that shit. Everyone has to account for his or her own actions and now you are accounting for yours, but if you really want help, we are here for you, don't bullshit us and waste our time. As far as Andrea goes, we will cross that bridge when we get to it."

We were all so caught up in Tom's conversation that we didn't hear the phone ring. Donna walked in and yelled, "Paul telephone," all we heard was "I can't believe this." After Paul slammed the phone down, I thought Donna was going to jump out of her skin. He noticed he had scared her, "sorry sweetie, why don't you go and sit down you've worked hard in the kitchen all day. I hate to be the bearer of bad news, but there is also some good news. It seems as if our sweet drunken mother and cracked out sister have gotten themselves arrested for shop lifting at Mr. Hall-More's store. Mr. Hall told me he wouldn't press charges on them because of our past history of doing business with him for years, as long as Anne and Andrea went into rehab and stayed out of his store when they finished there treatment program."

In a quiet voice, Donna said, "what else is going to happen? We can write a book and no one would believe us, it would be a best seller." Shannon suggested that they stay in jail. Paul said "wait, I have more news, Officer Michaels arrested Tony and Butch this morning around 2:30a.m coming of out of the club. Michaels said the look on Tony's face was as if he didn't care when told of his girlfriend's demise." Tony knew all the time that Jasmine was dead; he just didn't give a damn. "Thank god," we cried, and then we laughed. I've learned that laughing is the best medicine sometimes.

Donna was the only one that was not happy to hear the news. Donna interrupted, "I know that I might be out of line here but are you serious about leaving Anne and Andrea in jail?" Melvin still laughing, "yes, let them sweat it out for awhile, the funeral is in five days, get them out in four."

None of us had a problem with it; Darren had just walked in and was brought up to speed. It was getting late, we decided to have a grown folks sleep over. The telephone was ringing, thank god I have caller I.D, and it was nobody but Anne and Andrea calling from jail. I didn't answer the phone. Tom went to the store bought beer and wine coolers. We had a good time listening to music and dancing. All of a sudden, the doorbell rings, to my surprise it's Michael, Shannon's boyfriend. "I'm just in time." He wasn't going to spoil my fun, as I took inventory on him; he had good points, not many.

It was getting late; I had some sleeping bags that I pulled out for everyone. Everyone fell asleep except me. I decided to clean up the mess we made and clear my head. Thinking of what would happen next, I thought, as long as Andrea and Anne are not around, things will go smoothly.

I could feel someone watching me, so I turned around. Standing in the doorway was Darren with a smile on his face. "Darren you scared me I didn't hear you walk up." Can I join you?" he said with a smile. I could not help myself but to smile back. "Of course you can." We talked about everything that had happen this past week and what was in store for the future.

Darren slid his chair closer to mine, "Angelica ever since that night we went to the club, I can't get you off my mind." "Me to," I said with butterflies in my stomach. "Darren, I dream of you often to." I rubbed the side of his face with my hand. "I think you know what I'm saying Darren." He grabbed me by the hand, led me down in the basement and laid me on the couch. He slowly unzipped my shorts, pulling them down along with my panties. I had already pulled my shirt and bra off. He kissed me from my eyelids to m belly button. All the while, rubbing on my inserting his finger in and out of my pus making me hot and wet. He stoppe his pocket to make sure that he h Darren proceeded to lick aroun then going where most men the tip of his tongue and ran it across my clit. Goose bumps popped out, the size of cherries, a warm feeling engulfed my entire body. The more he licked, my hips begin to move. Darren opened my legs wider looking at me, "have you ever been tongue fuck before?" I got ready to answer him; before I could say a word he stuck his tongue into my cookie jar. He took my body on expeditions and journeys of pure pleasure, where they had never been before. I exploded with pure delight. Feeling the moisture on my face, I hear, "did you like that?" I just nodded my head up and down in a yes motion. Now here is the moment of truth, Darren unzipped his pants, pulled them down. The only thing that I could say, "CAPTIAN HOOK" and what was he going to do with that big thing. In the back of my mind, I'm thinking there are many brothers out here in the world who would love to have Darren's package.

I held his dick in my hand, stroking it ever so lightly. Massaging the tip, he laid his head back, closed his eyes and started a quiet moan. I laid a pillow on the floor and slowly entered his dick into my mouth; there is no shame to my game. I ucked and licked on his dick as if I were sucking a sucker to see if there was candy or gum he middle. The more I sucked the more he moaned. Darren pushed me away, with a smile on his face. Knowing that he was getting ready to cum, slid the condom on, laid me on the couch and entered me slowly. I had to bite my lip, I felt like a virgin all over again. The kid's dads were nowhere as good as Darren was. He was very gentle, my body adjusted to his quickly. Turning me over so I would be on top, I mounted that bull, rode him as if I was going to win a first place prize of a million dollars. We enjoyed ever minute of this, while licking and sucking on my nipples. He bent me over and did me doggy style, until we both had the ultimate climax. We laid there in each others arms, holding me tight, "thank you Darren, this is just what the doctor ordered, taking away all the tension and stress." Kissing me on my forehead, "there is more to come, this was just a sample." Thank goodness there was a bathroom down here. We washed up, making our way back upstairs and who do we see? Shannon sitting her ass at the kitchen table smiling from ear to ear. "I knew it was going to happen sooner or later. There's been an attraction between the two of you for years; your secret is safe with me."

Darren kept a fresh pair of clothes in his car, he wanted to take a shower and I had to sit down because my legs were still weak from our lovemaking. Shannon took my cup and freshened it up with coffee, making herself one. "Angelica was it what you expected it to be?" "My body is still tingling Shannon, that should tell you the answer." She agreed by saying "that just lets you know that it was good." Kelly walked into the kitchen "what are you two doing up?" Shannon and I started laughing; Kelly grabbed a bottle of water out of the fridge. "What is so funny?" Shannon told Kelly what had happen, "it's about time you and my cousin got your freak on, on that note, goodnight."

Chapter 4

I slept very well that night. I couldn't believe that this week had gone by so fast, sitting in the tub thinking about what was in store for us today, then again I cannot get Shannon off my mind, she's been here with me for the entire week. The morning after the sleep over Michael suggested that she stay with me, giving us some bullshit excuse that he has to work late and he doesn't want Shannon to be all alone in the condo. For that matter, she hasn't heard from him since then. I've asked about him, she just brushes me off and says that we would talk after the funeral. I'm thinking oh shit whatever she has to tell me must be serious, I'm just one person and at this point I can't take to much more.

I get out of the tub; I hear the rest of my family began to get restless because they wanted to get into the bathroom. I clean the tub out; go into my room to put on a pair of shorts and a tee shirt. I then go into the kitchen, pour myself a cup of coffee, a glass of orange juice and make myself a slice of toast. The phone starts to ring, "Good morning Moore residents'." On the other end a deep voice, "may I please speak to Angelica?" "This is she and to whom may I be speaking to?" "My name is Jimmy and I'm a friend of Damon's, I would like to know the funeral arrangements." "You say you're a friend of my brother? Well Jimmy, I know all of his friends and I've never heard of you before." "Angelica I do not live in Detroit, one weekend I was in town on some business, my car broke down and I had Damon tow it back to Ohio for me." "Oh I see, Jimmy do you have something to write with? The family hour is at 12:00 which is followed by the funeral at 1:00 at Pips funeral home, the address is 45 W. Blvd on the corner of James St." "Well thank you Angelica." "You're welcome Jimmy, make sure you come and introduce yourself." "I will do just that, goodbye."

Everybody came into the kitchen noticing the funny look on my face, I told them about the phone call I just received. We all felt that this just didn't sound right. I was getting ready to call

Darren, all of sudden I hear someone walking through the front door, it's Darren. I explained to him about the phone call from this person named Jimmy. I wanted to know had he ever heard of this Jimmy person. "No and as matter of fact we've never towed a car out of state." "Well he's supposed to introduce himself at the funeral." After hearing about Jimmy, Paul was uneasy so he called Officer Brown and told him about the phone call I received from this mysterious Jimmy person; he promised he would have a patrol car at the funeral home.

I went to get dressed; boy Darren looks good in that suit, trying to get my mind off the fact that in an hour or so we are going to bury my brother. Sitting on the side of my bed, I began to get butterflies in my stomach.

We are all dressed and waiting on the family cars to arrive. Melvin comes out of the kitchen eating some funky cheese burgers with extra onions, some sour cream and cheesy chips, Paul shouts, "get that funky shit out of here and why are you eating that now?" The only thing that he could say "I'm hungry." I told him, "go and brush your teeth and rinse your mouth out with some mouth wash." Oh God give me strength, here comes Andrea, Tom and Anne. To our surprise neither one of them were drunk or high. Tom decided to stay outside with the guys; Anne came in half ass speaking which didn't hurt my feelings.

Andrea walked up, gave Shannon and me a hug. We were blown away. "Thank you so much Angelica," for what Andrea?" "For showing me tough love." I hugged and gave her a kiss on the cheek, "you are welcome but I need to ask you a question, have you ever heard of a friend of Damon's named Jimmy?" "No, why do you ask?" I told her about the phone call. Anne had a strange look on her face and said, "Oh shit." I wanted to ask her if she knew anything about this Jimmy person.

The family cars pulled up. The drivers asked everyone to come into the house for prayer. They introduced themselves, "I'm Mr. Henderson, and I'll be your driver in the first car." I'm Mr. Barnes and I'll be your driver in the second car, is there a minister or a deacon in the house that would like to lead us in a word of prayer? If not the lead driver Mr. Henderson will lead us in prayer." Mr. Henderson proceeded, "LET US BOW OUR HEADS, HEAVENLY FATHER THANK YOU FOR WAKING US UP THIS MORNING AND KEEPING US IN OUR RIGHT MIND,

FATHER GOD BLESS THE MOORE FAMILY IN THERE HOUR OF NEED, KEEP YOUR LOVING ARM OF PROTECTION AROUND THEM, GIVE THIS FAMILY STRENGTH TO KEEP GOING BEYOND THIS DAY, WE KNOW THAT YOU ARE A GOOD GOD, WE KNOW THAT YOU DO NOT MAKE MISTAKES, AMEN."

In unison, we said, "AMEN," we were asked to line up. In the first car, it was Kelly in the front seat alone, Anne, Tom and Andrea in the back. In the second car, Paul up front, Donna, Shannon and myself in the back. Melvin decided to ride with Darren, Peewee, and Peanut, in the car behind us. Shannon spoke up, "did you see the look on Anne's face when you mention this Jimmy person to Andrea, Angelica?" "Yes and I can't wait to meet this person."

We arrive at the Pips Funeral Home at 11:45. All of the people that worked for Damon came with all the trucks washed and waxed with wreaths, roses and carnations in his favorite colors, burgundy and white hanging from the hoods.

We were lined up in rows of two's. Rev Cameron stood up at the microphone. "AND I HEARD A VOICE FROM HEAVEN SAYING UNTO ME, "WRITE, BLESSED ARE THE DEAD WHO

DIE IN THE LORD FROM HENCEFORTH. YEA, SAITH THE SPIRIT, THAT THEY MAY REST FROM THEIR LABOR, AND THEIR WORKS DO FOLLOW THEM.". I closed my eyes to talk to Damon "YOU ARE NOT ONLY MY BROTHER BUT YOU ARE MY FRIEND, YOU BRING BLESSINGS EACH DAY WHEREVER YOU GO, FRIEND, YOU ARE A PERSON THAT I'M GLAD TO KNOW, ONE WHO IS LOYAL AND TAKES TIME TO SMILE, WHO, WHEN THERE IS TROUBLE WOULD HELP OUT AWHILE, AN UNSELFISH NEIGHBOR WHO CARES HOW OTHERS FEEL, ONE WHO IS TRUSTWORTHY AND GIVES A SQUARE DEAL, A FRIEND, LOYAL TO GOD AND TRUE TO ALL MEN, A FRIEND WITH TRAITS OF A GOOD CITIZEN, YES, YOU ARE A PERSON THAT I'M GLAD TO KNOW, MAY GOD'S LOVE AND BLESSINGS ON YOUR LIFE BESTOW."

I went to sit down, I looked around to see if there was a face that I did not recognize, to know avail I did not see anyone I didn't recognize but I did see the police officers. All of sudden to our surprise, we saw walking in Monique, Serena, Sophia and a strange man. Looking at Mel, "did you know that they were coming?" He just shook his no. The strange man looks around and sees Anne in the front row and frowns. He walks up to me, "you must be Angelica?" "Yes and you must be Jimmy?" "Angelica can you and your family step into the lobby with me for a minute?" None of us knew why the girls were with Jimmy, I guess we were about to find out.

Once out into the lobby Jimmy spoke up, "you do not know me but I know all of you, my name is not Jimmy my name is James Moore and I'm your father." We all stood there with our mouths open not knowing what to say.

I still could not figure out why the girls were with him. James must have been reading my mind. "I want you to meet your stepsisters." Melvin turned white as a ghost. Serena looked at him and said, "Melvin we knew all along, that's why we never had sex with you. You could never pimp us and when dad saw you leave the house, he knew exactly who you were. Dad's been keeping track on you guys all of this time but because of Damon's death he had to come and show his respects." Andrea comes from the restroom casually walks by "hey dad" and walks into the chapel. We were all shell shock, Andrea knew and we did not.

Mr. Barnes steps out, "the funeral is about to start." James promised that he would explain everything later. I took my seat next to Kelly, she leaned over, "is everything ok?" I couldn't answer her, I was to busy looking at Anne as she just dropped her head. "I need a stiff drink and two cigarettes to tell you what's going on girl, we will talk later, as I turned to answer her.

Rev. Cameron asked if there were any remarks and please limit them to two minutes. Darren stood in front of the microphone and spoke the following words, *"DON'T THINK OF DAMON AS GONE AWAY, HIS JOURNEY HAS JUST BEGUN, LIFE HOLDS SO MANY FACETS, THIS EARTH IS JUST ONE. THINK OF HIM AS RESTING FROM THE SORROW AND TEARS. IN A PLACE OF WARMTH AND COMFORT WHERE THERE ARE NO DAYS AND YEARS. THINK OF HOW DAMON MUST BE WISHING WE COULD KNOW TODAY, HOW NOTHING BUT OUR SADNESS CAN REALLY PASS AWAY AND THINK OF HIM AS LIVING IN THE HEARTS. OF THOSE HE TOUCHED FOR NOTHING LOVED IS EVER LOST AND HE WAS LOVED SO MUCH."*

Darren lays his hand on the casket, "rest on my brother." Rev. Cameron asked, "Are there anymore remarks that anyone would like to make, if not would a Miss Carla Polk please come and read the obituary." Carla cleared her throat, *"DAMON MARCEL MOORE WAS BORN AUGUST 6th, 1977 IN DETROIT, MICHIGAN TO THE UNION OF JAMES AND ANNE MOORE. DAMON ATTENDED DETROIT PUBLIC SCHOOLS, GRADUATING FROM HIGH SCHOOL IN JUNE OF 1995, WHILE IN SCHOOL DAMON PARTICIPATED IN ALL SPORTS RECEIVING TROPHIES IN BASKETBALL AND BASEBALL. HE LEAVES TO CHERISH HIS MEMORY IS BELOVED WIFE KELLY, HIS MOTHER AND FATHER JAMES AND ANNE MOORE. THREE SISTERS, ANDREA, ANGELICA, AND SHANNON. TWO BROTHERS, PAUL AND MELVIN, ALL OF DETROIT. ONE NIECE AND TWO NEPHEWS. ONE BEST FRIEND DARREN A HOST OF OTHER RELATIVES AND FRIENDS."* Then she reads two poems. *"GOD LOOKED AROUND HIS GARDEN AND FOUOND AN EMPTY PLACE, HE THEN LOOKED DOWN UPON THE EARTH AND SAW YOUR TIRED FACE. HE PUT HIS ARMS AROUND YOU AND LIFTED YOU UP TO REST; GOD'S GARDEN MUST BE BEAUTIFUL. HE ALWAYS TAKES THE BEST;*

HE KNEW THAT YOU WERE IN PAIN HE KNEW THAT YOU WOULD NEVER GET WELL ON EARTH AGAIN HE SAW THE ROAD WAS GETTING ROUGH AND THE HILLS WERE HARD TO CLIMB, SO HE CLOSED YOUR WEARY EYELIDS AND WHISPERED PEACE BE THINE, IT'S BREAKING OUR HEARTS TO LOSE YOU, BUT YOU DID NOT GO ALONE FOR PART OF US WENT WITH YOU THE DAY GOD CALLED YOU HOME."

Carla had to wipe her eyes before she could read the last poem. *"WHEN I COME TO THE END OF THE ROAD AND THE SUN HAS SET FOR ME, I WANT NO RITES IN A GLOOM-FILLED ROOM, WHY CRY FOR A SOUL SET FREE, MISS ME A LITTLE BUT NOT TOO LONG AND NOT WITH YOUR HEAD BOWED LOW, REMEMBER THE LOVE WE SHARED, MISS ME – BUT LET ME GO, FOR THIS IS A JOURNEY WE ALL MUST TAKE AND EACH MUST GO ALONE, IT'S ALL THE PART OF THE MASTER'S PLAN, A STEP ON THE ROAD TO HOME, WHEN YOU ARE LONELY AND SICK AT HEART GO TO THE FRIEND WE KNOW AND BURY YOUR SORROWS IN DOING GOOD DEEDS MISS ME – BUT LET ME GO."*

The funeral director begins to close the casket; I thought I was going to die, knowing that I will never see my brother again. Kelly was the only one who did not break down. Rev. Cameron stood at the microphone "TO THE MOORE FAMILY, BE STRONG, KEEP THE FAITH AND HOLD ONTO GOD'S UNCHANGING HAND. TRUST IN HIM, LEAN ON HIM. I HAVE STOOD AT THIS PLACE SO MANY TIMES FROM THE YOUNG TO THE OLD, IT NEVER GETS ANY EASIER. I READ OF A MAN WHO STOOD TO SPEAK AT A FUNERAL. OF A MAN HE REFERRED TO THE DATES ON THE TOMBSTONE (1930-2000). FROM THE BEGINNING TO THE END HE NOTED THAT FIRST CAME THE DATE OF BIRTH AND SPOKE THE FOLLOWING DATE WITH TEARS BUT HE SAID WHAT MATTERED MOST OF ALL WAS THE DASH BETWEEN THOSE YEARS. FOR THAT DASH REPRESENTS ALL THE TIME THAT WAS SPENT ALIVE ON EARTH AND NOW ONLY THOSE WHO LOVED THIS PERSON KNOW WHAT THE LINE IS WORTH." FOR IT MATTERS NOT HOW MUCH WE OWN, THE CARS THE HOUSE THE CASH, WHAT MATTERS IS HOW WE LIVE AND LOVE AND HOW

WE SPEND OUR DAYS, SO THINK ABOUT
THIS LONG AND HARD. ARE THERE
THINGS YOU'D LIKE TO CHANGE? FOR
YOU NEVER KNOW HOW MUCH TIME
IS LEFT, IT CAN BE REARRANGED IF WE
COULD JUST SLOW DOWN ENOUGH TO
CONSIDER WHAT'S TRUE AND REAL
AND ALWAYS TRY TO UNDERSTAND
THE WAY OTHER PEOPLE FEEL AND
BE LESS QUICK TO ANGER AND SHOW
APPERICATION MORE AND LOVE THE
PEOPLE IN OUR LIVES LIKE WE NEVER
LOVED BEFORE. IF WE TREAT EACH
OTHER WITH RESPECT AND MORE
OFTEN WEAR A SMILE REMEMBERING
THAT SPECIAL DASH MIGHT ONLY
LAST A LITTLE WHILE. SO WHEN YOUR
EULOGY IS BEING READ WITH YOUR
LIFE'S ACTIONS TO BE REHASH, WOULD
YOU BE PROUD OF THE THINGS THEY
SAY ABOUT HOW YOU SPENT YOUR
DASH.

"LET'S BOW OUR HEADS IN PRAYER,
THIS IS THE DAY THAT THE LORD HAS
MADE, WE SHALL REJOICE AND BE
GLAD IN IT. DEAR FATHER AS WE SIT
HERE WITH OUR HEADS BOWED WE

ASK FOR PEACE FOR THIS FAMILY. LORD
WE KNOW THAT YOU ARE A GOOD GOD
A HEALING GOD. HEAL THIER HEARTS
DRY AWAY THE TEARS AMEN."

As the pall bearers carried the casket out of
the funeral home Rev. Cameron recites St. John
11:25-26, "I AM THE RESURRECTION,
AND THE LIFE: HE THAT BELIEVETH
IN ME, THOUGH HE WERE DEAD, YET
SHALL HE LIVE: AND WHOSOEVER
LIVETH AND BELIEVETH IN ME SHALL
NEVER DIE."

The ride to the cemetery took what seem like
forever, I could not believe that our dad was there
at the funeral, after not seeing him since I was
seven. I have three stepsisters that Mel tried to
pimp. The look on his face was priceless.

We finally arrived at the cemetery, Rev.
Cameron stood in front of me, "FOR I AM
ALREADY BEING POURED OUT AS A
DRINK OFFERING AND THE TIME OF
MY DEPARTURE IS AT HAND. I HAVE
FOUGHT THE GOOD FIGHT. I HAVE
FINISHED THE RACE, I HAVE KEPT THE
FAITH. FINALLY THERE IS LAID UP FOR
ME THE CROWN OF RIGHTEOUSNESS,
WHICH THE LORD, THE RIGHTEOUS

JUDGE WILL GIVE ME ON THAT DAY AND NOT TO ME ONLY BUT ALSO TO ALL WHO HAVE LOVED HIS APPEARING 2 TIMOTHY 4:6-8." I whispered to Rev. Cameron that I wanted to say something. Tears began to fall, "LIFE IS SO UNCERTAIN, DEATH IS SO UNKIND AND IT SEEMS THAT UNDERSTANDING IS SO VERY HARD TO FIND. A HAND HAS STRUCK, A LIFE IS GONE, WITH NO REGRET OR SHAME, WHETHER WITH INTENT OR ACCIDENTLY, THE END RESULT IS STILL THE SAME BUT FAITH WAS MEANT FOR TIMES LIKE THESE AND IF WE TAKE GOD'S HAND WITH LOVING WISDOM, HE WILL HELP OUR HEARTS TO UNDERSTAND."

I picked two red roses from the casket spray. Rev. Cameron sprinkled a hand full of dirt over the casket. "FATHER WE COMMIT THIS BODY OF DAMON MARCEL MOORE BACK TO THE EARTH FROM WHICH IT COMES FROM. ASHES TO ASHES, DUST TO DUST. FATHER LIFT THE BURDEN OF THIS LOSS WEIGHING HEAVY UPON THEIR HEARTS FOR THIS IS A SHORT SEPERATION. KNOWING THAT HIS

FAMILY AND FRIENDS WILL SEE HIM AGAIN ONE DAY IN YOUR KINGDOM. WITH YOUR RICHES AND GLORY. PEACE BE WITH YOU. THIS CONCLUDES THE SERVICES OF MR. DAMON MARCEL MOORE."

This has been a long day, I cannot wait to get home and get out of these clothes. We finally make it back on San Juan, people were everywhere, you had to ask them to move three inches in order to move one. I went into my bedroom, closed and locked the door, I hear Shannon, "open the door; I didn't know Damon knew so many people Angelica, he was truly loved." Shannon and I were changing clothes when she removed her blouse, what I saw made me want to scream. "Shannon what the hell happen to you?" "Angelica these are old wounds." "I don't care if they are old wounds, what happen?" "The night that Damon died Michael and I had a fight and he beat me with a whip." "Shannon, the kind that was used on slaves?" "Yes, promise me you won't say a word to anyone?" "Shannon I promise but this is not over with."

We went into the living room; Mrs. Peterson and her daughter out did themselves with preparing food. Anything you wanted was there from chicken cooked in every way, to all kinds of salad to corn beef. We will have food for days not to mention all the cakes and pies. People ate, drank and made plates to go. Friends came and went, they came in groves.

Everybody left, one thing about Mrs. Peterson and Linda they were both sweethearts, they cleaned up the kitchen. Paul was drunk by this time and this worried the hell out of Donna and myself. Paul took the last swallow of his drink, hemmed Michael between the wall and the front door, with his hands around Michael's throat. "Bitch I heard you cussing and yelling at Shannon the night we had the sleep over, if I hear that you've laid one hand on her, I promise I am going to kill you punk, do you hear me?" Darren had to pull Paul off Michael "Paul, man lets not do this, come on let's go outside and get some air." Michael grasping for air, "who in the fuck do you think you are Paul? Nobody says a word about you kicking Donna's ass when you feel like it." Paul broke loose from Darren, hitting Michael in the face. "Motherfucker I don't care if you are some so called attorney." Michael wiped the blood from his nose, charged Paul and the fight was on, breaking my end tables and lamps. Darren grabbed Paul and Melvin grabbed Michael.

Michael left before I could say a word, pissed off Paul grabbed Donna, "let's go and I mean right now." Her being the puppet that she is, jumped up and they left without saying a word. Paul's cover had been blown, for those who didn't know about the abuse, knew now.

I took a deep breath and said to myself, I'm not going to worry about this. Shannon spent the night with Kelly and I don't remember Melvin leaving. Therefore, that left Darren and me to clean up the mess of broken glass. We finished cleaning up, "Darren I really do not feel like being alone tonight will you stay with me?" He hugged and kissed me, "of course I will stay with you, I wanted to stay anyway." He locked the house up, went into the bedroom and cut the T.V. on. The house was very warm. The telephone rung, it was James "Angelica I am sorry for not showing up, I just didn't have the heart and I didn't want to see Anne, by the way can we make it for tomorrow at around 4:00p.m?" "That's okay James, I mean dad, I understand, 4:00p.m will be fine, good night."

Darren is a gem; he ran the shower until it felt warm enough. We showered together, he dried me off and I dried him off. Tonight was one night all we wanted to do was sleep. In a deep sleep, I heard the phone ring. "Hello, is this Angelica?" I replied yes. "This is Officer Roy over here at the Seventh Precinct." I sat straight up in the bed, turned the light on, and lit a cigarette. "We have your brother Paul Moore here in custody on charges of domestic violence against his girlfriend Donna, there is nothing you can do for him tonight, he has to appear before a judge, that will take place in the morning and at what time, I am not for sure, your best bet is to be at the courthouse around 9:00. This is when court opens up." "Thank you Officer Roy and goodnight."

Darren looked at me and asked what was wrong, I explained what happened, "damn baby I am so sorry." I just sat there in disbelief crying out of control. Darren put his arms around me to comfort me; I laid my head in his chest. God how much more can I take.

Chapter 5

I felt Darren get out of bed; turning over the clock on the nightstand, it read 7:00am. I could not help but to think about Paul. Knowing good and well that this was bound to happen. I was up and into the bathroom taking a long look at myself in the mirror. Stress was taking a toll on my body, so much has happened and it seems as if all of the problems are landing on my plate. I had to get myself together, wash up, and put some clothes on, only to hear the doorbell ring. Now who in the world could that be this time of the morning? Walking up front, there was Kelly, we said our good mornings and exchanged hugs, "Darren gave me the heads up on Paul and so what can I do to help?" "Right now Kelly I have no idea as to what to do, I guess we can just pray." We sat down for coffee. It seemed strange to see Kelly smoking before Damon's murder, I never saw her with a cigarette. I know I have the habit bad. With all she's been through, I understand why.

Joining us for coffee, Darren kissed me on my cheek, "don't worry I called the courts, they could not give me a specific time as to when Paul might go before a Judge named Borden.   It's best to be there as early as possible." Taking a puff off my cigarette and blowing smoke rings, I begin to feel that what happened to Donna was my fault, I had my suspicions that she was being beaten but I did not have any proof, until the day she came by here and I saw that she had an black eye, I remember telling her that she did not deserve to be beaten. I can't get the thought out of my mind of her reasoning for not calling the police on Paul, love!

Darren noticed I was deep in thought, "what's wrong baby?"

Taking my last puff and crushing the butt into the ashtray, "the day that Donna was hear I notice she had a black eye, I tried to call Paul to find out what was going on only to get the voice mail so I didn't leave a message. Then there was the day we made the funeral arrangements, I started to say something to him then but I got side tracked so there I go again not being able to talk to Paul.

Now he's been exposed thanks to Michael, so now he's sitting in jail and we don't know how she is doing." I became frantic; Darren's calming hand let me know that everything was going to be fine. "The only thing I know baby is that she's been admitted to Heavenly Hospital, they would not give me any information about her condition. You had nothing to do with Paul being in jail, he made that choice, which was a dumb one, to put his hands on that woman is certainly not the way to solve problems. Donna should have been smart enough to leave or gain a backbone to defend herself. So my love, do not beat yourself up over this." This is why I have Darren in my life; he knows just what to say. By the time we got ready to go, Princess Shannon comes walking in.

We met Andrea and Melvin in the lobby of the courthouse. We see the information desk; Judge Borden's courtroom was on the 18th floor, room 1816. We reached the 18th floor and by the look of the crowd, we were a little early and they hadn't opened the doors yet. Taking a seat on those hard ass benches to past the time, I told everyone James called to explain why he didn't come over to the house yesterday, and he would be there today at 4:00p.m. I turned to Andrea, "how did you know that he was our dad?" "I was at work one day and a man comes to me and asks me if I was Andrea Moore? I thought he looked familiar and I couldn't place the face. I told him yes I was Andrea Moore Wilson and could I help him? He then asked me if my mother's name was Anne. So again I say yes, by this time Anne pops up wanting to borrow money. She saw dad and asked him what in the hell was he doing here? You could tell he hated her, he said this is a damn post office; before I could intervene, he looked at Anne and said, you haven't changed one bit. You're still a drunk and I'm glad I left your ass. It was becoming a shouting match, so I took them outside; I didn't want my co-workers to see just how bad my so called mother looks. Anne was heated, she looked at dad and said I'm glad you left, you were sorry then and you're probably still sorry." So Shannon spoke up, "Andrea you never told us, why?" Andrea dropped her head, "let me explain, when you're on drugs you don't think about trivial things like that, then you and Angelica were excluding me out on things, its like you didn't have time for me, so why tell you? I would try to get up the courage to call but changed my mind, so I said the hell with them; I know it's because I'm using these damn drugs that you exclude me from everything, then to Shannon, you think you're so much better then everyone else, so I figured if you guys wanted to know about dad you would find out on your own."

Melvin patted Andrea on the back, "big sis, I'm so proud of you, finally saying out loud to us that you use drugs." "Melvin I'm not proud of myself, you were too young to remember any of this, Angelica and I use to see Anne drink and sleep with so many men when dad was not at home. I made a vow that I would never do any of the things she did, now look at me I am worse off then she is. So me being proud, no."

We were finally able to go inside the Courtroom, once again sitting on even harder ass benches. This tall older looking man approaches us, "are you the Moore family?" Extending his hand to Shannon, "yes we are the Moore family and you are?" "I'm Mr. Timothy Brantley Sr. from the Law Offices of Brantley, Barnes and Jackson; I'll be representing your brother Paul." Shannon was turning into bitch mode, "so how is Paul, Mr. Brantley?" "The arresting officer said that Paul did not resist arrest last night and he appeared very remorseful. I understand that you all just buried your brother yesterday and I am sorry for your lost." Shannon not missing a beat, "Mr. Brantley I know good and well that you are not going to use the excuse that we just buried our brother as his defense?" Before Mr. Brantley could respond to what Shannon had said, the bailiff stood, "all rise, the Honorable Judge Borden presiding, Mr. Brantley scurried along to the defendant's table. Judge Borden was a nice looking man who seemed to be fair looking. The bailiff brought Paul out and stood him next to Mr. Brantley. Judge Borden adjusted his robe, "you may be seated. Good morning, as you know I am Judge Borden, before I begin I would like to say this, I am a fair judge and I listen to all my cases carefully, once I make my rulings there will be no out burst, do I make myself clear." All you heard was a wave of yes. The bailiff handed Judge Borden a file. "Docket case number 1682019926, the State of Michigan vs. Paul Moore on one count of domestic violence." Judge Borden took a sip of water, cleared his throat and before he could say anything Mr. Brantley stood, "your honor if it may please the court?" Judge Borden waved his hand, "you my proceed Mr. Brantley." Your honor I have consulted with my client Mr. Moore, he does not want to drag his family through this or embarrass them any more then what he has already done, he wishes to plead guilty to the charge." The judge adjusted his glasses then rubbed the bridge of his nose, "before I proceed does anyone know the condition of the allege victim?" Mr. Bridge the attorney for the state stood, "your honor she is doing very well and will make a full recovery." Well Mr. Moore you have entered a plea of guilty, and this is your first offense, it burns me to see men like you beat on women. Mr. Moore do you have any children, especially daughters?" Paul in a low voice, to the point that we almost couldn't hear what he had said, "no sir." "Now Mr. Moore run with me on this, how would you feel is some man were beating on your mother, daughter, or sister? You wouldn't like it would you?" "No sir I would not." "Well this is someone's daughter and sister. Mr. Moore this is your first offense, I sentence you to one year, no more then nine months in the county jail. I strongly and I do mean strongly suggest that you take anger management classes while you are there and when you are released, I order that you take these same classes every Saturday for one year, after one year you will be evaluated, we take violent crimes very serious, I am aware that your brother's funeral was yesterday and he died from a random act of violence. Is there anything else you would like say?" Paul dropped his head, "no sir and thank you." The judge slammed his gavel down and said next case.

Out in the hallway we agreed to go and see Donna. We arrived at the hospital. The information clerk would only let two of us go up at a time. Kelly and I went first. Arriving in front of her room, we both took a deep breath and walked in. I wanted to cry; there Donna was lying there with a broken leg and arm. Her eyes were swollen shut from the beating Paul gave her; also her face was purple and blue. She must have sensed that I was there, with her left hand she waved for me to come to her. Tears were running down both of our faces, as I approached her bedside Donna grabbed my hand as tight as she could. "Donna sweetie yes it's me Angelica and I have Kelly with me. Donna we just left the court, Paul pleaded guilty to the charge; the judge gave him one year no less then nine months. He has to take anger management classes while in jail, also when he comes home he has to take them every Saturday for one year."

Donna was trying to say something, Kelly walked up, "Donna honey please do not try to talk, things are going to be okay, I promise you, we've gotten over one hurdle, we can get over another." I kissed her on her hand, "when you're released you are going to stay with me until you get better, Kelly and I are going now. Shannon and the gang are waiting to see you."

On the elevator, "Kelly I am coming apart at the seams, my stomach is always nervous when ever the telephone rings, I've become a nervous wreck." Kelly was calm most of the time; she's been like that from the first day I met her, "Angelica you have to have faith and trust in the lord with all your heart, God is the super glue that will hold you together." "I can't do this anymore Kelly," "yes you can Angelica, and there is no such word as can't."

Shannon and Melvin went up next, Darren and Andrea decided that they wouldn't go up. Therefore Darren went out to smoke a cigarette and use his cell phone. I could tell there was something on Andrea's mind, "Andrea are you okay?" We all went and sat in the corner "Angelica, Kelly, I feel so stupid these drugs have caused me to do things that I never thought that I would do, it has torn my family apart and has destroyed my marriage." Sliding closer, "honey Tom loves you so much and yes he has told us everything from you losing your job to what you have done with Tony and Butch" and he has forgiven you, he just wants the two of you to get some help."

Darren walked in just as Shannon and Melvin were getting off the elevator; we all sat there for a minute, Shannon started yawning, "I feel you Shannon, we all need to go and get some rest, James is going to be at the house at 4:00p.m." We all stood up to leave, Darren stopped us "I received a telephone call, our attorney called and he wants to meet with us this evening around 8:00p.m for the reading of Damon's will."

Looking at him with a funny look on my face "I did not know that Damon had a will." "The first draft of the will was drawn up when we opened the business and when Kelly and he got married, he had the will amended." I rode in silence on the way home not knowing what to say. I noticed that Andrea could not sit still, "Andrea are you alright?" "To be honest Angelica, no I'm not alright, I need a fix bad but I am not going to get one, I'm going to quit cold turkey, I have to do this." I told her I as so proud of her. "Can I spend the night with you? There are a lot of things I want to talk to you and Kelly about." This sounded serious, I just wanted to go home and take a nap.

I could hear the telephone ringing when I stuck the key into the lock. I ran to the phone almost falling over the ottoman. "Hello Big Cedric and how are you?" "I'm good baby; I heard about Paul, are you okay?" "I'm well as can be expected." "Well Angelica if there is anything that I can do just let me know. I do mean anything, if you want me to cook dinner or rub your feet and back, I'm your man." "Thank you Cedric with your nasty self, but I'll be ok and furthermore I have a man that can do that for me." "Ok baby, the real reason that I called, you've been through so much these past few weeks, I want to keep the boys the rest of the summer, you're a damn good mother and I need to pitch in more." "Cedric do you really want to do that for me? that would mean a lot to me." Not a problem Angelica we are having a ball and it feels good to hang out with them, plus they are a ladies magnet." Well once again thank you Cedric and tell the boys that I will talk to them later."

Since Cedric was going to keep the boys the rest of the summer, I decided to call Byron and see if he would keep Denise as well. Dialing the number, I was hoping that his mother would not answer the phone, I liked her a lot but she could talk your ears off. Damn, "hello Mrs. Douglas and how are you?" "Hello sweetie, I'm good. Mrs. Douglas is a small woman with a big loud voice; I go on to ask her if Byron was at home. "No baby,

Byron is not here, he took Denise to get an ice cream cone. Is there something I can help you with?" "Yes Mrs. Douglas, my brother Paul is in jail and you know Damon's funeral was yesterday. This is why I'm calling, is there any possible way that Denise can spend the rest of the summer with you guys? I would appreciate it if it is not too much trouble and if you can't I understand." "Now Angelica you know it wouldn't be a problem at all for her to stay and I know Byron wouldn't mind, I'm really enjoying Denise, so honey you get you some rest and I'll have Denise call you later, bye." I sat on the side of my bed thinking Cedric and Byron, they are pretty good fathers.

Looking at the clock on the nightstand it was just 1:45p.m, I had time to take a nap, I hear Darren come into the house walking in the room, "what are you up to?" Me being a smart ass, oh 5'4 and 125 pounds." We both laughed, "Well Shannon, Kelly, and Andrea are in the living room sleep, and I want you to do the same thing. Melvin and I will hold things down." I turned onto my stomach, the phone rung again, Darren answered it, the only thing I heard him say was ok and that he would give me the message. Tapping me on my shoulder, "that was James calling to cancel and he promised to be here tomorrow."

That was fine by me, all I wanted to do was get some sleep but what was James so afraid of, right now I really didn't care. Sleep was coming over me fast and before I went out like I light I told Darren about the conversation with the kid's dad, whatever Darren said was a blur, I was knocked out.

I woke up to Miss Shannon jumping on my bed, "wake up, come and eat" "Shannon what time is it?" "It's 7:30." "Ok let me go to the bathroom and I will be right out." She followed me in and closed the door. "I want to ask you something, can I spend the night here tonight?" "Of course you can and why would you ask, you're my sister and I love you? We grew up in this house together through the good times and the bad." "Angelica I just thought that you might have company and didn't feel like being bothered with me." "Never that, plus Andrea wants to spend the night as well, she wants to talk and says it's very serious. Now will you please leave so I can pee in peace?"

Walking in the kitchen drying off my hands, the smell of Chinese food made my stomach tap dance with delight. Melvin had ordered the whole menu. We said grace and chowed down, by the time we finished eating and cleaning up the kitchen the doorbell rung. It was Damon's attorney. "Kelly let him in and introduced him." "Mr. Lee I would like you to meet the Moore family." He shakes all our hands and takes a seat across from me. He removed a folder from his briefcase. "This is a legal and binding *will* if any of you feel this is not right, you have the right to petition the court to contest the *will*. This is the *will* of Damon Marcel Moore so dated June 3, 2005. The *will* reads." **I DAMON MARCEL MOORE BEING OF SOUND MIND AND BODY, LEAVE MY WIFE KELLY MOORE THE DEED TO THE NEW HOUSE, THE NEW CADILLAC DTS, ALL STOCKS AND BONDS FOR BOTH COMPANIES, NET WOTH OF 5.5 MILLION DOLLARS.**

TO MY OLDEST SISTER ANDREA, I LEAVE YOU A PAIR OF 2 CARET STUDDED DIAMOND EARRINGS, 500,000 IN CASH WHICH SHANNON WILL OVERSEE, PROVIDED YOU AND TOM GET SOME HELP AND PROVE THAT YOU CAN STAY CLEAN FOR TWO YEARS. TO ANGELICA I LEAVE YOU MY 2005 HUMMER, MY HOUSE, ALSO I LEAVE YOU 500,000 IN CASH. TO MY SISTER SHANNON I LEAVE YOU 500,000 IN CASH AND MY OTHER

PAIR OF 2 CARET STUDDED DIAMOND EARRINGS.

TO MY BROTHER PAUL I LEAVE YOU MY CONDO IN NEW YORK, PLUS 500,000 IN CASH. TO MY BABY BROTHER MELVIN I LEAVE YOU THE RENTAL PROPERTY THAT I HAVE ON SAN JUAN, MY 2005 MUSTANG AND 500,000 IN CASH BUT BEFORE YOU RECEIVE ANY OF THESE THINGS, ANGELICA WILL OVERSEE YOUR ASSITS UNTIL YOU GET A REAL JOB. TO MY BROTHER IN-LAW TOM I WOULD LIKE YOU TO WORK FOR THE COMPANY, STRICKLY LIGHT DUTY, I ASLO LEAVE YOU 500,000 IN CASH PROVIDED YOU MAINTAIN YOUR SOBRIETY FOR TWO YEARS, AFTER WHICH YOU WILL RECEIVE YOUR ASSETS. DARREN WILL OVERSEE THESE ASSETS UNTILL YOU ARE ABLE.

TO MY ONE AND TRUE FRIEND DARREN WHO HAS BEEN LIKE A BROTHER TO ME, I TURN OVER MY CONTROLING INTERESTS IN THE COMPANY TO YOU. I KNOW YOU AND KELLY WILL DO A WONDERFUL JOB, MAKE ME PROUD AND IF PEEWEE AND PEANUT COME

AROUND LOOKING FOR WORK THROW IT TO THEM. TO MY MOTHER ANNE I LEAVE YOU 100,000 IN CASH AND KELLY WILL OVERSEE YOUR ASSETS UNTIL YOU MAINTAIN YOUR SOBRIETY FOR TWO YEARS. AFTER SUCH WHICH TIME YOU WILL RECEIVE THESE ASSETS. TO MY NEICES AND NEPHEWS I LEAVE 100,000 IN AN ANNUITY THAT MR. LEE WILL OVERSEE, IN THE EVENT THAT MR. LEE RETIRES HE WILL APPOINT A NEW ATTORNEY.

TO MY FAMILY I GUESS YOU ARE WONDERING HOW I OBTAINED ALL MY ASSETS. OVER THE YEARS I'VE MADE SOME VERY WISE INVESTMENTS AND I HOPE YOU DO THE SAME, MAKE YOUR MONEY WORK FOR YOU AND DON'T WORK FOR THE MONEY, WITH ALL MY LOVE DAMON MARCEL MOORE."

We sat there cried and said thank you to Damon. Kelly walked Mr. Lee to his car, coming in she handed us one of his business cards. We looked at each other, no one knew what to say, Melvin dropped his head into his hands, "I can't take this anymore I'm out of here, this has been too much for me. First my brother is killed, then at his funeral I learn that the three girls I've been trying to screw are my stepsisters and now my brother Paul is in jail for beating the hell out of his girlfriend.

Tom pats Melvin on his back, "man it is going to be alright, we all know that Damon was a giving person and that he would give a dog one of his kidneys if he knew it would save his life." What Tom said was true, Damon was a giving person and he would help anyone who was trying to help himself or herself. Melvin kissed me on the forehead telling me he was leaving; Tom decided to spend the night with Mel.

Kelly handed me an envelope that was addressed to Darren as we excused ourselves and went into the bedroom. My hands were shaking, what in the world could this be? I opened the envelope, it was a letter from Damon. I read it aloud, "DEAR ANGELICA AND DARREN; THERE ARE SOME THINGS I WANT YOU TO KNOW. FIRST, I'VE KNOWN FOR A WHILE THAT THE TWO OF YOU HAVE FEELINGS FOR EACH OTHER. IT'S COOL THAT MY BEST FRIEND AND SISTER ARE TOGETHER. I KNOW DARREN WE BROKE THE CODE. I ALSO KNOW THAT YOU WILL DO RIGHT BY HER; SHE WILL

DO RIGHT BY YOU. MY NEICE AND NEPHEW LOVE YOU DARREN, YOU LOVE THEM. THEY'LL HAVE THE BEST OF BOTH WORLDS WITH YOU AND THERE DADS. DARREN YOU KNOW WHAT TO DO. I'M THERE WITH YOU AND WILL BE WITH YOU THE REST OF THE WAY. ANGELICA KEEP AN EYE OUT FOR KELLY SHE NEEDS YOU."

MUCH LOVE DAMON

With tears in my eyes, I looked at Darren, he stood and walked to the dresser, opened the drawer and turned to me getting down on one knee "Angelica make me the happiest man alive and become Mrs. Darren Simpson." He asked me for my left hand and slid a two and a half caret princess cut platinum ring on my finger. With tears rolling down my face, I said, "yes!" Kelly, Shannon, and Andrea were hollering and screaming so loud that you thought they were getting a ring.

He leaned down, kissed me on my neck, and whispered in my ear, "lady you know that you owe me some good loving, I know that your sisters want to talk to you and Kelly, so I'm going to go and chill with Melvin and Tom and I'll see you in the morning." Walking him to the door arm and arm, I gave him a kiss, "bye ladies," before they could say good-bye, he had closed the door.

Celebrating my engagement to Darren, the girls and I decided to have drinks of champagne and orange juice, which tasted very good. We were having a good time, I could not help but to think what Andrea wanted to talk to us about. She pretended to be having fun; we all noticed the look of despair in her face. I knew she was going through withdrawals, "Andrea is there something wrong, you look as if you are about to cry, I know that you wanted to talk to Shannon, Kelly and myself so what's up?" "Angelica I don't want to spoil your moment," "Andrea now come on you aren't going to spoil my moment so spit it out." There we go again another envelope; I opened the envelope, what I read I wished I had never asked. I went into hysteria, Kelly had to calm me down "I can't believe this Andrea, tell me this isn't so." "Angelica I'm afraid so, I have full blown AIDS."

I must have fainted; I was stretched out on the couch with a cold pack over my forehead. I opened my eyes; no I was not dreaming. Shannon was holding Andrea in her arms as if she were a baby doll. Sitting up trying to get myself together, Andrea turned to me with a tear stained face, "Angelica I'm so very sorry that I spoiled this time for you. I knew no other way to tell all of you this, I found out a couple of months ago, I knew something was not right, I began to get lesion on the back of my tongue and by not having any insurance I went to the free clinic, they did the entire test and they called me in a few days ago and gave me my results. I know this is going to destroy my marriage, Tom has no idea, and I hope and pray to God that he doesn't have it. He's been a good man to me and I've done this horrible thing to him. I have no idea as to whom or how I contracted this terrible disease. I've been in the streets for a long time and at the clinic they wanted me to give them a list of names of all the men and or women that I've had sex with in the last year, whether it was intercourse or oral. The list is well over 80 people combined."

Chapter 6

Time has flown by so fast, its August already, Damon has been dead two months and may God rest his soul. As for my family, Andrea told Tom she has full-blown AIDS, he's filed for divorce. Thank God they're both in drug treatment and doing well with that. Shannon left Michael, she caught him in bed fucking another woman, and she tried to put him out but couldn't, so she just left. She moved all of her things into storage and now she is living with Kelly.

Melvin is working hard with Darren, Kelly is doing fine and we both are back doing hair full time in my basement. Life has to go on. Donna is being release from the hospital today, having several surgeries but will make a full recovery. She agreed to stay with me until she feels as if she can live on her own. Darren moved in with me and the kids, Melvin sold Damon's house and bought Darren's house. Haven't seen much of Anne lately, she went by Kelly's house drunk as hell trying to get her money from Damon's *will*, Kelly wouldn't budge on giving her the money, so I guess Anne is still mad.

James has called numerous times to say he was coming over but he never shows up and at this point we don't care. We receive letters from Paul twice a week. In his last letter, he mentioned something about coming home in December, something or another about the jail being over crowded and they are doing some early releases. He still has to do his anger management classes every Saturday from 8:00am to 2:00pm.

Donna says that if she takes him back they would have to go to marriage counseling. None of us knew that they were married. Since James would not come by here, Sophia called and said she was going to stop by around 7:00pm. The kids are doing fine having fun with their summer over their dads. I am going to visit with them on Sunday. With all that has happen I still have restless nights.

I've been doing hair all day so I can't wait until the shop finally closes to go upstairs and relax; here comes Kelly and Shannon with Donna. We are settled on the couch; Melvin and Darren come in with a pizza. I told them that Sophia would be here any minute. Before we could finish our last bite of food, she walks up on the porch and Shannon lets her in. We say our hello's and she takes a seat right next to Melvin, "first of all thank you for meeting with me, I know dad has made promises of coming over but he calls and cancels. To the best of my ability I am going to explain how we are stepsisters, she took a deep breath, when dad and Anne got married she was already pregnant with Andrea, things were going good, dad was working at the auto plant, and Anne was a seamstress. By the time Andrea turned two, Anne learned that she was pregnant again, dad was excited about having another baby girl but Anne wasn't happy.

When she gave birth to Angelica, Anne felt tied down having two small children, dad worked long hours and on his day off would go to the pool hall and have a few beers, shoot pool or play darts, which pissed Anne off and she felt like dad should've been at home to relieve her to do whatever she wanted to do. Therefore, in the daytime she would go to the liquor store and buy whiskey and cigarettes, so when the girls went to bed at night she would drink. Dad told me when he came home, Anne was already asleep and the more he would go out the more she would drink. By the time Angelica turned two, once again Anne learned she was pregnant this time with your sister Shannon, dad's job had laid him for a few months and things only got worse. All Anne wanted to do was drink but couldn't because she was pregnant, so all they did was argue. Shannon was born and the lay off was longer then what dad expected, now that the baby was born, she went back to drinking. Anne had kids ages 2, 4 and a new born. Dad went on to explain that the more your mother would drink the more he stayed out at night. He said he couldn't take it anymore, all the drinking was getting on his nerves and he left. He would come by to see you guys and have sex with Anne, then he would leave, he didn't want to be with Anne if she couldn't stop drinking. He told me he loved her very much and was willing to give it another try, he came back home when your sister Shannon turned two. Anne wasn't drinking and things were ok. Dad says things got a little crazy the day she found out she was pregnant with your brother Paul; her world fell apart. Dad told her while being apart, he had gotten another woman pregnant and I'm that child. Your mother was quite upset over dad's infidelity but blamed herself, so she forgave him and made attempts to try and work things out. According to dad Anne wanted to meet my mother and tried to convince him over and over again but he refused every time. After many tries, she just gave up. When Paul turned two your mother was pregnant with your brother Damon, dad said that he was overjoyed to have three daughters and two sons but your mother felt something was just not right but she couldn't put her finger on it. She needed someone to talk to so she called her sister Katie who had just relocated here from Georgia.

Katie would tell Anne that she was crazy for thinking that dad was doing anything wrong. After forgiving him the first time why would he cheat on your mother again? Katie would tell your mother what a good husband dad was and how much he loved his kids. She found out later he had another baby on the way, my sister Monique. Anne was so upset she told dad to leave. After your brother Damon was born Anne really begins to drink. To everyone's surprise dad and your mother never divorced. When your brother Damon turned two, Anne needed some help with the children so she called dad at work, he came by the house so they could talk. Dad told me after your mother promised that she would stop drinking and dad promised to stop being promiscuous they should give it one more try and work things for the kids' sake and once again dad came back to your mother. Dad said that your mother would have one drink at dinnertime. Anne was pregnant once again with your baby brother Melvin and everything seem to be fine until Anne went to the grocery store one day and overheard some women talking about dad had yet another baby on the way with another woman, which would be my sister Serena. Anne never opened her mouth to dad to reveal that she knew about this new child. Once again Anne felt that she had brought all this on herself because of her drinking. Things were going well,… so dad thought, until one-day he came home early from work only to discover Anne having sex with the man from across the street. Dad told me she had made you all stay in the basement, this really pissed dad off that she would have you guys in the basement while she was upstairs having sex, no respect for you guys at all he felt. That's when he left and never came back. Therefore, you see me and Paul, Damon, Monique, Melvin and Serena we are all the same age. Anne did some investigating on her own and found out that the woman dad had these kids with was your Aunt Katie, my mother."

My eyes grew bigger then car tires, all of our mouths flew open in shock. I managed to say, "this is some fucked up shit you only see on T.V. talk shows." Sophia continued, "dad concluded this was the reason why Anne drank so much, her only sister had betrayed her and in her eyesight this was not acceptable. My mother knew Anne would never forgive her. My mother was always jealous of Anne; she wanted everything Anne had, the husband and kids. Anne always confided in mom, when Anne and dad would fight, dad would come over to the house and talk to mom about Anne and somehow things went too far."

"Dad got comfort from mom when Anne would put him out and mom liked this. This is why you guys never saw much of mom when you were growing up. My mother became very distant from your mother after we were born because my mom wanted dad to herself. So mom sat down and wrote Anne a long letter to explain everything, Anne got so upset that she told mom that they were no longer sisters. Mom had a nervous breakdown, then one day she just walked off and left us, leaving dad to take care of us all on his own." Listening to all that Sophia had just said I looked at her, "don't sugar coat this shit, James was fucking two sisters at the same time and didn't care if this shit would tear them apart or not, he just didn't give a damn. One is a drunk and the whereabouts of the other one is unknown." "Angelica you're right I'm not trying to make excuses for dad; they all were wrong. No one would ever know that we were brother and sister because there isn't much resemblance between Anne and mom they had the same mother but different fathers, that's why Mel had no idea that we were related when he met us at the club. I guess you are wondering why my sisters and I became dancers, we got older and dad couldn't handle us anymore plus the money is good and it pays for me to go to school, as for my sisters I guess they dance for the hell of it." Sophia stood to leave, "I've overstayed my welcome, and thank you for allowing me to do something that dad didn't have the heart to do." I walked her to the door, "Sophia don't make dancing a career." "Please believe me Angelica I won't." I then told Sophia to give us time to let all this sink in and that I would call her later. "I understand Angelica, maybe one day we all can get together and let by-gones be by-gones."

Donna spoke up and said "this is a big pill to swallow." Darren patted Melvin on the leg, "I guess your pimping days are over with now." I had a headache out of this world. As I walked away I said, I SWEAR YOU WOULDN'T WANT TO BE IN MY SHOES.

I woke up in a cold sweat and I must have jumped up because Darren cut the lights on and said, "are you okay?" "I must have had a bad dream, I'll be ok." I couldn't go back to sleep. I looked at the clock on the nightstand; it was 4:30a.m. "Angelica do you want to talk about it?" "Darren you have to be up in a few hours, I'll be alright, go back to sleep."

I went into the bathroom to wash my face and brush my teeth and I stood there looking in the mirror, reflecting on all what's happened. I began to cry so hard that I almost didn't hear the knock at the door. I open the door and Donna was standing there, "I heard you crying, come and sit with me and let's talk for awhile."

"Donna do you want a cup of coffee?" As I was walking to the kitchen, "Angelica sit down, I'll get it, and yes I know I just came home from the hospital, I need to move around so I won't get stiff." A few minutes later she came back with coffee and slices of pound cake. "I know Angelica we've never really sat down and had a real conversation, I know what you are thinking, yes I love Paul with every fiber of my being, I don't know what I'm going to do and yes I've endured a tremendous amount of abuse but I do believe with God's help, I'll be given the right direction. Angelica we'll get through all of this, Shannon will get over Michael and the fact that she caught him in bed with another women, she has to learn how to soften up a little and stop being so hard, Kelly will get over Damon's death, we have no idea how she is feeling we've never lost a husband, Andrea and Tom will beat this devil called crack Andrea chose the life that she did now she has to deal with the fact that she has full blown AIDS and that she will die with, I hate to sound so harsh but fact is fact and bullshit is bullshit. Anne will one-day wakeup and say I've had enough of this liquor I want no more. Darren will be a good husband and stepfather to the kids I feel this in my bones. Angelica you can't bare all of this weight on your shoulders, let some of it go, and most of all try to find a way to open your heart to Sophia, Monique and Serena, none of us asked to be here, that was your parent's pleasure."

"Donna you don't understand everybody comes to me with there problems." "Angelica sometimes you have to tell people in a nice way that you don't have time because you have three kids of your own to worry about. Since I've known you Angelica you've always found time for family, whether it's to lend an ear, a shoulder to cry on or a place to stay and as far as friends are concern, answer this question for me, when was the last time you went to a friend with a problem?" Did they make time for you and don't count Kelly?"

I sat there sipping my coffee thinking about what Donna had just asked me and I couldn't think of one person. "So Donna your saying that I'm soft? Oh God no Angelica, you're a strong black woman raising three kids on your own, but you put other peoples needs before your own. It's time for Angelica." In the back of my mind I'm thinking that Donna isn't dumb as a bag of rocks. "Now let's take Mark and Anthony for an example Angelica, when they have boyfriend problems they come to you and cry on your shoulder. You'd listen and open up your heart to them, when you and Byron broke up and you needed someone to talk to, neither one of them had time for you. Mark had company and Anthony had a new love interest. Now let's talk about Tammy and Carla, the two drama queens, did you tell them that you were engaged to Darren, if you didn't just wait and see how they act when you tell them. My advice to you is to watch them, remember this; all friends are not true friends." We talked so long, that I didn't notice Darren getting ready to go to work. We said our good mornings, he kissed me and we exchanged our good byes. Darren looking back "do you ladies need anything before I leave?" At the same time Donna and I said "no thank you." Both us were sleepy we decided to get some sleep.

Chapter 7

I needed a distraction after hearing Tony's trial would start on the 21st of August so we took the kids to the movies then for pizza. It felt so good seeing them, they jumped up and down when they saw my car pull up. As always Cedric and Bryon were very understanding for keeping the kids until after Labor Day. To my surprise I learned that Cedric and Carlos were expecting a baby sister. Big Cedric gave me a hug he then congratulated me on my engagement to Darren. We both deserved some happiness.

I pulled into the driveway Shannon and Kelly were standing there patting there feet as if I was in trouble. "Angelica where in the hell have you been I've called all over west hell looking for you?" "Sorry Mother Shannon and Kelly I had to get out of the house, the last thing I wanted to hear from you guys is about Tony's and Butch's trial starting soon and I don't want to be there, I just want to hear that they got the same guilty verdict."

The only thing that I hated was that Darren had to testify; he was there and saw the whole thing, I worry about his safety. Then again I knew Darren could handle himself in any situation, he was no coward, all I can do is just pray and keep the faith like Donna and Kelly told me to.

Buster walked in the house with Melvin, "well hello Buster, haven't seen you in a while and why didn't you come to the funeral, I mean what's up with that?" "Angelica I know, I know I'm guilty as sin and I know I haven't been over to see you and the family, you know baby girl that I don't do funerals and it hurts my heart to know that Tony did this foul ass shit. I hate to say this, I hope him and Butch rot in hell, let me stop, I didn't come over here to make you guys feel sad. I saw Mel in the store, he gave me the heads up as to what was going down with the Moore family, and all the shit you guys have been through blew my wig back. These doors to this house have been open to a lot of people for many years and I hope more years to come. Baby girl and cookie can we talk in private?" These are the names that he gave

Shannon and I when we were kids. We walked out onto the front porch. "Listen you guys it's more to it then Damon's passing why I haven't been by here. I felt some of you were mad at me because of what happen with Andrea and Tom with that crack shit. You've known me for years and I've thrown a lot of parties and I've invited all of the Moore family to these gigs. I hope you guys don't think I allow these kinds of drugs in my house." I just wanted to let you all know that I checked the shit out of the person who brought that shit to my pad; they will never come to my crib again. When I got wind of what was going on that night, I shut the party down and put everybody ass out."

"Buster, Shannon and I are not blaming you for Andrea's and Tom's stupidity, I'm quite sure no one put a gun to their heads and made them smoke crack cocaine. Buster we could never hate you for what they did, it is now up to Andrea and Tom to get themselves together, but Andrea has a major strike against her, not only trying to stay off the glass pipe but she has full blown Aids." Baby girl before I go I'm having a backyard party tonight and I want you all to come and if Donna get's too tired she can stay in my room until you all are ready to go." I gave him a hug and said that we would be there.

I went back into the house, and my entire family was looking gloomy, "what's wrong." Mel handed me the calendar and pointed, "what's today's date? Not realizing it was Damon's birthday, I just sighed and said happy birthday little brother. Donna was being more vocal, not being the shy and timid person like she usually is, "let's not be sad and remember we are to rejoice when someone dies and we are to weep when someone is born, so we're not going to sit her looking like sad sacks. We're going to get ourselves together and go to this party and enjoy ourselves, do I make myself clear." We all looked at Donna and said yes mom.

We arrived at the party, it seemed like the whole neighborhood turned out, people were dancing and the liquor was flowing, making our rounds none of noticed that Melvin was talking to Buster. We hear Buster on the microphone, "may I please have your attention, thank-you for coming to my last party for the summer, but on a serious note folks there's someone who's not here to enjoy the festivities and I hope no one minds taking a moment of silence to remember our departed friend Damon whose birthday is today and there is another reason to celebrate this evening, the engagement between Angelica and Darren, now let's raise our glasses and congratulate the newly engaged couple, Angelica and Darren."

In unison we hear congratulation, here comes Tammy and Carla running over to hug me and the first thing Tammy did was grab my hand to see the ring. "Damn Angelica, Darren must really love your ass, look at the size of that damn rock on your finger." I looked in Donna's face and remembered what she told me about so-called friends, (Everyone who smiles in your face may not be your friend.) She mouthed the words, "watch your friends." All the while Carla kept asking, "why didn't you tell us?" "Calm down Carla it just happened a few days ago." "So have you set a date yet?" Before I could answer Carla, here comes the drama queen Tammy saying, "you know me and Paris have been talking about getting married, so we can have a double wedding Angelica," in the back of my mind I'm thinking, no the hell we can't have double wedding.

Before I could say anything Kelly came up to me, "excuse me can I borrow Angelica for a minute?" I gave the girls a phony smile as we walked away; I turned around and saw both those hoes whispering. I knew those bitches were not my true friends. "What's wrong Kelly?" "I hope that there isn't going to be any trouble because Brenda's ass is here." Damn this is all I needed, thank goodness Shannon was dancing with our friend Richard. Brenda saw Shannon, she then grabbed a friend of ours named Lorenzo and made him spill his drink on Tammy's white Capri pants.

Brenda was bumping and grinding so hard on Lorenzo he began to get a hard on. For his own sake, it was dark outside, if it had been light out, we would have thought that he wore a strap on, a sock or that the brother was truly blessed. Finally Shannon sees Brenda glancing at Buster, with a nod of the head, Shannon knew what to do. Brenda had her back to Shannon, she tapped her on the shoulder, Brenda turned around, "hoe I told you that revenge is the best dish served cold." Shannon slapped Brenda so hard that she looked as if she had spun around twice, knocking her off balance. The partygoers backed up to give them room. Running up was Lisa and Nicole, Brenda partners in crime, not too far into the distant was Shannon's crew Angie, Tracey and Cora. Not even a man or woman wanted to go up against Cora. Cora is a big bitch; she stands six feet tall, wears a size twelve shoe, to see her she looked like a sex change gone wrong but was cool as hell.

Brenda must have taken some I'm bad pills; she shoved Shannon, which just made Shannon laugh which terrified her. Standing behind Brenda were her friends, seeing Cora walk up made them change there minds. Leaving her to defend herself, one swing was all it took to knock Brenda down, one stomp was all there was to leave Shannon's 5 ½ shoe size footprint embedded in the middle of Brenda's face. Waiting for her to get up, Shannon took a sip of her drink. On all fours, then upright, Brenda hauled ass. The crowd hollered Buster grabbed the microphone "we have a winner the undefeated champion, bookworm and the loser that is hauling ass, hood rat hoe."

I looked around to see that Carla had Darren are hemmed up in the corner, rescuing my man from the claws of this barracuda, "come on baby lets dance griming Carla, "now come on Angelica you don't trust one of your friends talking to your man?" Giving her the once over look, "don't you know that if you play with sharks you are bound to get bitten." I smiled at Carla and walked away with my arm around my man.

The party was ending, we were saying our goodnights "Buster you have to come by the house sometime and we just shoot the shit, and have a couple of beers." Kissing me on my cheek, "sounds good to me." Approaching the house, getting a closer look, I see Paul sitting on the porch eating pizza. Donna's body was stiff as spray starch, wanting to know what he was doing here, Shannon jumps from the car before it came to a complete stop. "Paul no one knew that you were coming home this soon, did it occur to you that you should have picked up a phone and called first before you came here?" Shannon was throwing questions at Paul so fast that he did not see her walk pass. Paul throwing his hand up, "hold on Shannon you are asking me too many questions, first of all, I wrote Angelica a letter telling her that it was a possibility that I would have a early release. Second I called the house but there was no answer, I couldn't remember the cell phone numbers."

Walking into the house, Paul handed Miss know it all Shannon his release papers. "Paul it says here that you have to do one year of anger management classes every Saturday and damn it Paul you are going to go. Paul could sense that Shannon was mad, hurt and bitter with him, "ok Shannon I see that you are upset so let me have it both barrels." "Paul I know that you answered these questions in court but I am going to ask you them again. How would you feel if your daughter had a man that was kicking her ass all the time, has it dawned on you that Donna is somebody daughter?" Paul started crying, "just stop it Shannon I get it, looking at Donna, "honey I am so sorry for all the hurt that I've put you through, I love you so much and I will never put my hands on you in that way again, I will do what ever it takes to win your trust love and respect back." Donna went and sat next to Paul, "let me ask you this, how in the world can you beat on a women that you claim that you love so much? never mind you don't have to answer that question, I will tell you this, I can honestly say that I have no idea of what is to become of this marriage, you should be grateful that you are out of jail and so you won't get any ideas, I'm staying her with Angelica and Darren. I won't come home with you and I don't want you to try and spend the night, nor come over everyday unless I call you and invite you over. I know that this is not my house but you said that you would do what ever it takes to get me back, well actions speak louder than words, so prove it to me." Paul dropped his head, "I can respect that and I will grant you this."

I am so proud of Donna she's finally got a backbone. We sat there in total silence not knowing what to say, so Paul broke the strange silence, "I have a question what in the hell is going on in this neighborhood? I saw Brenda hauling ass down the street." We started laughing I told Paul what happened. We started laughing again. Coming back to reality "Paul there is so much more that I need to tell you. He sits up in his chair, giving me his undivided attention. "I'm going to make this short as possible. There was a reading of Damon's *will;* you were left his apartment in New York, and 500,000 in cash. The girls that Melvin tried to pimp, well it turns out that they are our stepsisters and their mother is Aunt Katie. Andrea and Tom are in drug treatment, Andrea learned that she has full-blown Aids and as far as Anne goes, we haven't seen her. Tony's trial starts August 21st and Darren has to testify, we've all agreed not to be there, we just wanted to know the damn verdict. Last but not least, Darren and I are engaged." Paul tried to absorb and process all this information, he begins to cry, and his cries sounded like it came from the pit of his soul. Donna wanted to console him, I touched on her knee and whispered in her ear "let him be, he has so much to cry for."

Chapter 8

Everything is almost back to normal. I can't believe Thanksgiving is in a couple of days. Cedric and Carlos are in a latch key program thanks to there father, Denise is taking a dance class that her aunt runs. I've been doing hair all day since the holidays are approaching and my damn hands hurt. Shannon agreed to stay with Kelly until the New Year, Donna and Paul are going to marriage counseling but Donna is still living with Darren and I. Paul spends every other weekend with us, I still haven't seen James yet. He finally called and told me how embarrassed he was to talk face to face. I told him what happen all those years ago between Anne and Aunt Katie didn't concern any of us, we were his children and all was forgiven. I wanted him and the girls to come over for Thanksgiving dinner. I promised to call him the next day to tell him what time.

Kelly comes in the house yelling, "where is everybody?" crushing out my cigarette, "Kelly what is going on, you are out of breath, let me get you some water, are you okay?" Taking slow sips to catch her breath, "I didn't want to say anything until I was for sure, I'm 5 months pregnant and I am sorry for waiting so long to tell you, with all that was going on I didn't need to be stressed out." I'm truly happy for her; I know Damon would be elated. Kelly had brought me out of my thoughts "Angelica your so called friends are out on the front porch" Shannon being herself, "let them bitches wait' I hear Tammy's smart ass." "Damn Angelica, I know you're engaged and all, with your fly ass ring and all but do you just leave your girls out in the cold?" quick tongue Shannon, "what do you fake ass bitches want? We have not seen you since Buster's party, Carla with your whorish ass all up in Darren face, bitch get a man of your own, I never did like you neither one of you, the only reason why I put up with you is for my sister's sake, you are not true friends. You only come around for free hair dos. Speak your business and get the fuck out. Or are you hear to tell us that you and Paris are getting married Christmas Day? that's the rumor going around. Well honey you know I went to high school with Paris, I ran into him at the drug store so I had to congratulate him. He just laughed and told me that the 3 ½ caret C.Z. that you are wearing on your finger right now, you bought from his mom out of her jewelry magazine. He also went on to explain that you had him mistaken and he wasn't going to marry you. He said and I quote, "Tammy was just a easy piece." By the way he said if I run into you, when are you going to pay his mom her money for that ring. Just like Brenda, you can't turn a whore into a housewife. I think I've summed you two tricks up, so if there is anything you have to say better say it now then get the fuck out." There was nothing for them to say Shannon had pulled their hoe card. They knew not to go up against Shannon they saw what happen to Brenda and they didn't want that to happen to them. So they just picked up there cracked faces off the floor and walked out.

I laughed so hard, my side was hurting. The guys came in wanting to know what was so funny, rehashing the current events, they were happy to learn that Kelly was pregnant and that James and our sisters were coming to Thanksgiving dinner. We need to get to know them, after all their last name is Moore. I saved the best for last, Andrea will be here from treatment and we must treat her the same. Shannon tapped her fingernails on the table to get our attention. "There is something that I need to get off my chest. I know that I have been bitter here lately, and for that I apologize you all don't know the true nightmare that I have been through lately with Michael. He has been abusing me physically, verbally and emotionally, he has even beat me with a whip, and to top it all off, I caught him in bed with two women Tammy and Carla that's why I truly do not like them. So I left Michael. I've been staying with Kelly and if I know Angelica she wanted to tell you, but I wanted to tell you myself, I needed to hear it out loud. That's why I was so mad at Paul for treating Donna the way that Michael treated me, totally disrespect. So to you all I am truly sorry and I love you all with all my heart."

Holding back my tears and emotions, "ok you guys go and do something because you will only be in the way and we have food to prepare." I'm busy picking greens, I hear Melvin say oh shit, "Anne is coming." Lord give me strength, I really don't need this. I cannot take her now. To all of our surprise, she was sober and looked good, like her old self. I gave her a hug, "where have you been? I haven't seen you since the funeral." "I have been in A.A. for the past several months, I know what's been going on, Carla's mother Vivian was in treatment with me, and when ever Carla came to visit Vivian she would pass the news on to me," so I know about Shannon catching Tammy and Carla in bed with Michael, I also know that Andrea and Tom are in rehab, he filed for divorce and she has full blown Aids. I'm glad you know about your stepsisters, I just couldn't talk about it when you kids were younger. I understand I'm going to be a grandmother Kelly is pregnant. Donna and Paul are married and you and Darren are engaged. Shannon let me tell you this, you are a pretty girl, you are smart and the right man will come along and sweep you off your feet, just keep the faith. This is going to be a Thanksgiving that I will never forget, now you all come and give me a hug because momma loves all her kids." For once we were a family.

Chapter 9

Another six months have passed; I cannot believe all that has happen. I don't know where to begin, let's see its Anne's birthday; the family decided that we were going to surprise her at her apartment with ice cream and cake. Knocking on the door several times with no answer, hearing the television in the background, we had the manager let us in only to discover she had died in her sleep from natural causes. Kelly gave birth to a healthy baby boy named Damon Marcel Moore Jr., we call him DJ and the both of them are doing well. Tony and Butch were both sentenced to life with no chance of parole, so those sons of bitches will never see the streets of Detroit again. Shannon has truly changed her ways, she is now in a serious relationship with Harvey aka. Peanut, after all these years I've never known his real name. The two of them are very happy and much in love no wedding date has been set yet. I've not seen my so-called friends since that day Shannon went off on them at the house. I do know that Anthony has moved to Georgia with his new boyfriend, and that Mark, his job moved him to New York as a fashion designer for theater. Donna and Paul are doing well, they are expecting there first child sometime in the winter. Tom completed the drug treatment program and is doing real good, he divorced Andrea, and she completed the program as well but dealing with the fact that she has full-blown Aids, she relapsed but this time her drug of choice was Heroin. In the beginning she was snorting the drug and ended up shooting the drug. One night she overdosed and was found dead in a vacant house on the eastside with the needle still in her arm. Now my sister and I get together once a month for lunch and a day at the spa. We finally opened the beauty shop, called Anne's place. Sophia received her degree in criminal justice; Monique and Serena are still dancing at Cupcakes. Melvin kept his promise and he is still working with Darren. As for myself, Darren and I are no longer together it was just not in our cards. I thought that when you date someone you accept them for who they are and their faults. There were things I didn't like about Darren but that was my man and I had to accept those things. I guess there were things that he couldn't accept. In the beginning of our break up, I will admit that I was hurt but I remember him telling me once that he doesn't see breaking up as a bad thing. In the department of breaking up, women handle that differently than men. I think Darren did love me and was in love with me in the beginning, he had to be he asked me to marry him. I do know that I was in love with him from the first day we became a couple, a woman knows how she feels and I will always love him. The day he walked out of my life, he told me that I was his best friend and that will never change. I found out later on he had a girlfriend, a baby on the way and they were a couple when we were together, typical of a man. I'm now a manic depressant and having an emotional breakdown is what sent me over the edge, dealing with all that has happen in my family and my children were killed in a car accident while coming home from a friends birthday skating party. The friend's mom was driving and a semi truck ran through a red light slamming into the car. The impact killed them instantly. I haven't seen my family in a while but I do keep tabs on them and how they are doing. Well diary I haven't slept nor have I showered in four days and I look and smell terrible. My nurse is knocking on my door it is time for my medication before I shower and get ready to see my shrink in my new home at the state mental hospital. I hear gunfire on the television, I have a flash back and I think to myself whoever that is. I wouldn't want them to be in my shoes.

Signing out

Angelica D. Moore

2:27pm

About The Author

I was born and raised in detroit michigan. I am the only child. Writing short stories came to me at an early age. I still reside in detroit with my life time partner and my daughter

Printed in the United States
85762LV00001BA/25/A

9 781434 308795